FRONTIERSMEN

Volume 12

True Tales of the Old West

by

Charles L. Convis

PIONEER PRESS, CARSON CITY, NEVADA

Library of Congress Catalog Card Number: 96-68502

ISBN 1-892156-02-4 (Volume)
ISBN 0-9651954-0-6 (Series)

Printed by
KNI, Incorporated
Anaheim, California

CONTENTS

ILLUSTRATIONS

LAND OF HIS OWN

They were called long hunters, men who left home for months, even years at a time to search for game and adventure. Daniel Boone was the greatest of them all. Daniel was twenty-one in 1755 when he served in the Colonial Militia under George Washington. The next year he married sixteen-year-old Rebecca Bryan. Just after their third child was born, Daniel crossed the mountains into Tennessee on his first long hunt. His younger brother, Ned, agreed to look after his family. When Daniel returned twenty months later, Rebecca had a new baby.

"Whose is it?" Daniel asked.

"She's Ned's," Rebecca replied. "You were gone so long and the other men came back but no word about you. I didn't know if you was still alive. Ned came to comfort, and he looked so much like you, and, you know — "

"What's her name?"

"Jemima Boone."

"Well, if the name's the same, I guess it's all the same."

Daniel always treated Jemima like his own. She went with him everywhere, even after she married and had children of her own.

Daniel fought at Blue Licks, Kentucky, in the last battle of the Revolutionary War. Daniel's men fought well, but the other two leaders blundered. Israel Boone, the second son of Daniel and Rebecca to be killed in the war, was the last man buried in that conflict.

Daniel continued to develop the dark and bloody ground he had first explored. But with claims to a hundred thousand acres of Kentucky land, he went broke and lost everything.

In 1799 Daniel, already a legend in Kentucky, moved on west to the Spanish lands beyond the Mississippi. Daniel, nearing sixty-five, and Rebecca looked forward to a new start where a brave man could wrest land from the wilderness. Daughters Jemima and Susannah and their families followed.

The new land — present Missouri — was governed by Spain, but most of its people were French trappers. Daniel started out with 850 acres for himself, with the power to distribute about 350 additional acres to each of his followers. He selected rich bottomland on the north bank of the Missouri River, about sixty miles above its mouth. Soon the government asked Daniel to bring in another hundred Kentucky families, giving him 8500 more acres for himself and

Rebecca.

Napoleon's dream of restoring France's colonial empire soured. He convinced Spain to return the land and then sold it to the United States. With the United States doubled in size, the man most responsible for pushing the frontier across the Alleghanies now led followers further west.

But first came the question of the new American government confirming land titles. Daniel had learned the importance of preserving paperwork after his bitter experience in Kentucky. But his papers were signed by the lieutenant governor in St. Louis, not the governor in New Orleans. And he had not cultivated any land as required by Spanish law. "I'm a hunter," Daniel said, "not a farmer." He lost it all.

But it was not so bad this time. His sons still had their land, and the country was full of game. Also, there were more lands to explore to the west. He traveled to the Rocky Mountains and the headwaters of the Missouri. Soon the leading explorers of America's new land — William Clark, Meriwether Lewis, Zebulon Pike, Manuel Lisa — were stopping by to pay their respects and seek Daniel's wise counsel.

He tried to enlist in the War of 1812, but the government thought seventy-seven was too old for a soldier. His sons and grandsons served instead.

During maple sugaring in 1813, Rebecca died. She was in the woods boiling sap at the time. She had spent fifty-seven of her seventy-four years as Daniel's wife. Daniel buried her on a high cliff above the Missouri.

Daniel's son Israel had been killed after the British had surrendered in the Revolutionary War, but before the news reached Kentucky. Incredibly, Jemima's son, James Callaway, was killed after the peace treaty ended the War of 1812, but before the news reached Missouri. By then Daniel was living with Jemima.

Daniel was still exploring the Dakotas and the Rockies well into his eighties. He even talked about going to California. It was not to be. The greatest frontiersman in our nation's history died in 1820, a month short of his eighty-sixth birthday.

The bodies of Daniel and Rebecca now lie in a graveyard overlooking the beautiful Kentucky River in Frankfort. It is the only piece of land that could ever be called Daniel's own.

Suggested reading: Lawrence Elliott, *The Long Hunter*, (New York: Reader's Digest Press, 1976).

A ROARING SOUND, LIKE THUNDER

Josiah Wilbarger and his young bride emigrated from Missouri to Texas in 1828. After two years in what is now Matagorda County, they moved to the Colorado River, ten miles above Bastrop. There Wilbarger built a cabin for his wife and baby. The closest cabin to the Indians, it was called the sentinel cabin for civilization in that area.

In August, 1833, Wilbarger and four other settlers were surveying land about six miles east of present Austin when sixty Indians attacked. The Indians killed two settlers outright. The other two escaped, ignoring Wilbarger's pleas to help him up on one of their horses and take him with them. Wilbarger had already been shot once with a gun and twice with arrows.

Poor Wilbarger's good as dead, the escaping men thought as they galloped away.

The yelling Indians closed in on Wilbarger, shooting him again with a rifle picked up from one of his dead companions. The shot into the neck paralyzed him.

Then the Indians stripped and scalped each of their three victims. Wilbarger was fully conscious during the scalping, although he could not move.

"I couldn't feel a thing," he said later. "When the knife sliced around my head, I heard a roaring, sort of, like the sound of thunder."

Wilbarger lay in a dreamy, semi-conscious state until late that evening. Then the pain from his many wounds brought him alert, craving water. He dragged himself to a spring and lay in the water until the chill lessened the pain. When he was so numb that he feared he would die, he crawled out to dry land and went to sleep.

He woke up under the hot sun, blow flies crawling in his wounds. He drank from the spring and caught some snails, which he ate raw. He struggled to his feet and headed toward Joe Hornsby's cabin, downstream on the Colorado. He staggered a quarter of a mile and fell, exhausted, at the foot of an old post oak tree.

In the meantime, the two men who escaped reached Hornsby's. A messenger hurried to other cabins for help. Considering the number of attacking Indians and the fact that all three men were presumed dead, the settlers at Hornsby's decided to wait until help arrived before returning for the bodies.

Wilbarger spent a long and agonizing night under the

post oak tree. He was delirious much of the time. He kept seeing visions of his sister, Mrs. Margaret Clifton, who lived in St. Louis County, Missouri. He could even hear her voice as she spoke gently:

"Brother Josiah, you are too weak to get back alone. Stay here and friends will come to aid you before the setting of another sun."

Wilbarger saw and heard his sister clearly. He was puzzled how she could be with him when she lived seven hundred miles away. When her voice stopped, the apparition moved off in the direction of the settlements.

Wilbarger called out piteously: "Margaret! Stay with me." But she vanished into the night.

That same night, Mrs. Hornsby woke from a vivid dream. She told her husband that she saw Wilbarger alive.

"He was naked and scalped and lay at the foot of an old tree," she said.

"Impossible," Hornsby said. "Go on back to sleep."

She slept fitfully until three, when the dream returned. She woke her husband again and said they should go to Wilbarger's rescue at once.

"I saw him again," she insisted. "He's not dead. I'll fix breakfast so we can get a good start."

A relief party of Mr. and Mrs. Hornsby and a few of their neighbors left early that morning. They found the two dead men. Then they heard Wilbarger's feeble voice.

"Don't shoot, friends, it's Wilbarger," he said. As they ran toward him, he collapsed, whispering, "water, water."

When Wilbarger was revived, he told of seeing and talking to his sister. He still believed that he had seen her in person, and he could not understand how she had got there from Missouri. The settlers buried the two dead men and carried Wilbarger back to Hornsby's. After a few days of Mrs. Hornsby's careful nursing, the wounded man returned to his own cabin. He recovered and lived twelve more years. He left his widow and five children a handsome estate.

Several weeks after Wilbarger returned to his own cabin, a letter brought sad news from Missouri. Margaret Clifton, Wilbarger's sister, was dead. She had died the day before the Indians attacked her brother.

Suggested reading: James T. DeShields, *Border Wars of Texas* (Tioga, Texas: The Herald Company, 1912).

GAUNTLET AT PAWNEE ROCK

Pawnee Rock, a four-acre rock formation southwest of Great Bend, Kansas, has seen many fights between Indians and frontiersmen. One of the earliest was an attack by sixty Kiowas against Jim Gibson and his partner, Bill, in 1836. Gibson told the story to Kit Carson, who passed it on to Major Henry Inman.

Gibson and Bill had been trapping and were packing their pelts out. They had picketed their mules on the west side of the rock and had climbed to make their camp on top when the Indians attacked. The men weren't worried at first. They had plenty of powder, a pouchful of bullets each, and two jackrabbits for food.

The Indians circled the rock, gradually closing in. Arrows fell like hail but missed their mark. When the Indians came too close, the trappers fired, making each bullet count. In late afternoon some Indians on foot tried to remove the bodies of their fallen tribesmen. The trappers' volleys forced retreats. At dusk the Indians withdrew to a makeshift camp. A few patrolled around the rock to prevent escape.

After dark, Gibson slipped down to the prairie to get buffalo chips for fuel. Back on top, he built a small fire and they cooked rabbit. After the meal they moved their mules closer to the top, where they found some fresh grass. They worried that neither they nor the mules had any way to get water. They also worried about the Indians smoking them out by setting fire to the tinder-dry prairie.

Their worst fears came true shortly after daylight, when the Indians moved northwest and started the fires. Gibson moved the mules to the east side, where the rock wall was the highest. He hoped the flames and smoke would pass over the animals as the fire raged toward the rock.

Huge clouds of smoke rolled upward. The sun tinted them bright crimson as the wind drove the fire along. The men crouched under a rock overhang, and were soon enveloped in darkness. A sheet of flame passed close to where they huddled.

Then, as if by magic, the sky was blue again. Through watery, smoke-filled eyes the men watched the fire pick up speed and roar away to the southeast. Two Indians, trying to steal the mules, misjudged the fire's speed and were engulfed. Gibson said it was a horrible sight, even though they were enemies.

The fire sped on to the Arkansas River, leaving behind the blackened carcasses of coyotes, crows, turkeys, grouse, and wolves. It jumped the river and continued on. Gibson thought it had traveled eight miles in fifteen minutes.

The Indians approached to make sure the trappers were dead. The volley of shots caused a surprised retreat. Then the Indians tied their horses together, covered them with branches and lodgeskins, and began driving their moving fortification toward the rock, walking behind in safety.

Gibson and Bill began shooting horses. After a few had fallen, the Indians were confused. Some continued toward the rock without the protection. The besieged men made every shot count.

Finally the Indians withdrew, but the men were almost out of ammunition. A lone Indian, carrying a white blanket, walked forward, making the peace sign. He said they knew how brave the two trappers were. They wanted them to come to their camp, where they would be treated kindly and adopted into the tribe. Gibson and Bill refused the invitation.

The Indians mounted their horses and charged the rock. The trappers soon fired their last cartridge. They stacked loose stones into piles. Then the brave with the white blanket again rode forward. This time he suggested a race, giving the Great Spirit of the white man a chance to prove its life-saving power. Gibson and Bill had no choice; they accepted the challenge.

The knife gauntlet ran for two hundred yards, starting at a cottonwood tree on the Arkansas River bank and running out into the prairie. One man would run it; if he made it, both would go free.

Each trapper said he would be the one to run. Gibson insisted, saying he had run a similar gauntlet after capture by the Apaches, and their knives had never struck him.

About thirty Indians had survived the battle. The chief positioned them on both sides of the race course. Each brave waved his scalping knife aloft.

Gibson stepped forward to run, but the chief shook his head, and pointed to Bill.

Bill stripped to his drawers. The chief gave the signal, and Bill sprang forward like an antelope. The Indians yelled and slashed with their knives. Bill struck some of the warriors, pushing them away, as he fled down the course. He escaped unhurt.

The two men walked back to Pawnee Rock, loaded their mules and headed east. From their camp that night on the north bank of the river they could hear the Kiowas chanting the death song for their fallen warriors.

Suggested reading: Henry Inman, *Stories of the Old Santa Fe Trail* (Kansas City, 1881).

BIGFOOT WALLACE

William Alexander Wallace came from a distinguished Scottish family. Ancestors included the great Highland fighters, William Wallace and Robert the Bruce. His father was the first territorial governor of Florida.

In 1836 Wallace, then twenty, went to Texas to avenge the killings of his brother and a cousin, a West Point major, by Mexicans in their slaughter of prisoners at Goliad. He got there after the Texian victory at San Jacinto, but he stayed to "take some pay out of Mexicans."

He joined a party on its way north to survey and locate land along Palo Pinto Creek (present Palo Pinto County west of Fort Worth). On October 23 they reached their destination and began setting up camp. The next day Wallace decided to have a look around. A party of twelve or fifteen Indians chased him. He killed the man in front (his first Indian) and then fled. He wasn't worried about getting caught. "I could run like a scared wolf when I let out the kinks," he said. But he had no idea where he was when the chase ended.

He wandered for five days, spending one night in a cave while a storm passed. Then he sprained his ankle and couldn't walk for about three weeks. He hobbled back to the cave, where he lived on venison, turkey, pecans, and berries.

He came to a substantial stream on November 21. (Later he thought it was the Leon River, southwest of the Palo Pinto.) The next morning at daylight he was surrounded and captured by a large band of Comanches.

A giant of a man for those times, Wallace stood six feet two, had a six foot six reach, and weighed 240 pounds. An old Indian woman, as "wrinkled and ugly as an old witch," took a liking to him. After the warriors bound him to a stake and heaped wood all around him for execution by fire, the woman pleaded for his release. Other women rushed past the warriors, untied Wallace, and turned him over to the old one. Wallace lived with the tribe for three months, and then escaped with the aid of Black Wolf, an adult son of his adopted mother.

Wallace returned to the settlements at LaGrange, then moved to Austin and on to San Antonio. He spent much of his time scouting for Indians on the frontier. In 1842 he fought against Mexicans who captured San Antonio and then retreated south of the Rio Grande. Later that year Wallace and about 230 Texians made a retaliatory attack at Mier.

Outnumbered ten to one, the Texians were captured.

On their forced march south, Wallace and others escaped, only to be recaptured again. On March 25, 1843, to teach the prisoners a lesson, the Mexicans decided to execute every tenth man. They put 176 beans in a covered jar, seventeen black, the rest white. Those who drew black beans were to be shot.

The officers drew first. One of them noticed that the black beans had been poured in last. "Dig deep, boys," he passed down the line. Only one officer drew a black bean.

The men drew in alphabetical order. Twenty-four white beans had been drawn in succession when Wallace's turn came. He thought his chances were pretty slim, but he had stood close while the drawing proceeded, and he thought the black beans may have been slightly the larger. After carefully feeling under the covering, he drew out a white one. The next two to draw got black ones.

The next day, as the lucky men resumed their march, they filed past the "bloody and stiffened forms of their murdered companions." They were imprisoned just outside Mexico City. Some of the foreign residents of the city provided clothing for the prisoners. They had to get specially-made shoes for Wallace, who wore number twelves. For the rest of his life he was called Bigfoot.

Bigfoot Wallace and three others were released in August, 1844, as a result of a petition to Mexico from the United States Congress. Bigfoot returned to Texas and joined the Texas Rangers. His company distinguished itself at Monterey in the War against Mexico.

"I reckon my accounts with the Mexicans are about square," Bigfoot said after the battle.

Bigfoot's impressive appearance, his humor, and an almost childlike simplicity in describing his exploits, despite being a literate man who could read well, made him one of Texas's most famous heroes. He never married, although he once had a "leaning" to Alice Ann, whom he described as a blue-eyed, partridge-built young woman.

In spite of Indians and Mexicans, Bigfoot Wallace lived to age ninety-two. He is buried in the state cemetery at Austin.

Suggested reading: John C. Duval, *The Adventures of Big-Foot Wallace* (Philadelphia: Claxton, Remsen, 1971).

BIGFOOT WALLACE

The Daughters of the Republic of Texas Library

JOHN BOZEMAN

Montana Historical Society, Helena

TRAIL FINDER

Mining gold in Montana's Grasshopper Diggings that first winter of 1862-63 was tough. John Bozeman, 25-year-old Georgia native, looked for an easier way to make a living. The first prospectors had come from Colorado and California gold fields, but most of the men still to come would follow the Oregon Trail west. That way was a long one, requiring two crossings of the continental divide. A short cut would take four hundred miles off the journey.

Bozeman turned to veteran frontiersman John Jacobs to ask, "You reckon we could find a more direct way with grass enough for horses and oxen?"

"Might could. Be a bunch of hostiles, though. Them Blackfeet's always on the warpath."

Bozeman looked down at his rough hands and worn boots. He'd grown more callouses than he'd found nuggets. "Let's give it a try come spring."

Their search took them over the pass from the Gallatin Valley into the Yellowstone Valley. They followed that valley down to the Big Horn River, where they turned southeast. Staying east of the Big Horn Mountains, they crossed the headwaters of the Tongue and Powder Rivers, reaching the Oregon Trail well east of the continental divide.

They had to fight Indians while locating the shortcut. During the short time the Bozeman Trail was open it was bloody from constant warfare. The army built three forts to protect it. John Bozeman guided emigrants over the shortcut and did some packing of his own.

In 1867 Bozeman and Tom Cover headed down the trail toward the military forts. Cover, one of the discoverers of gold at Alder Gulch, had a flour mill and he hoped to sell supplies to the military. Bozeman went with him to plead for military help in resisting Indian attacks near the gold fields.

Bozeman and Cover left the Gallatin Valley on April 16. They climbed the pass and followed the Yellowstone River toward Forts C. F. Smith and Phil Kearny. On April 20, while resting in their noon camp, they saw five Indians approaching. They were in the country of the Blackfeet and Sioux (both tribes hostile) and the peaceful Crows.

"They're Crows," Bozeman said when the Indians were about a hundred yards away. "I recognize one of them. Let's let 'em come on. Maybe they'll know where the Blackfeet and Sioux camps are."

Cover wasn't sure; he kept his Henry rifle handy. The Indians came closer. They raised their hands and repeated, "Ap-sar-ake, Ap-sar-ake (Crows)."

Suddenly Bozeman spoke, "I'm fooled, Tom. They're Blackfeet. Hand me your rifle real easy and then go and saddle the horses. If we're careful we may get out of this mess yet."

Cover followed Bozeman's suggestion. As he finished saddling his horse, he saw an Indian drawing the sheath from his rifle. "Shoot, John," he hollered.

But Cover's rifle jammed, and an Indian shot Bozeman in the chest. As he fell, another shot also struck his chest, and a third Indian shot Cover in the shoulder.

Cover ran to Bozeman. "Are you badly hurt, John?" he asked, picking up his rifle. He didn't hear a reply as he worked desperately to get the rifle to work. Three Indians advanced on him and the other two ran to the horses.

Cover retreated about fifty paces toward a willow thicket before he could open fire. One Indian dropped dead and the others ran to the two who were saddling Bozeman's horse.

Cover, fearing a renewed attack, retreated further into the willows. He stayed there an hour and then saw the Indians crossing the river. They rode the saddle horses and carried their dead warrior on the pack horse. Cover returned to the camp and saw that Bozeman had certainly been dead when he hit the ground. In their haste to steal the horses and escape, the Indians had neither scalped him nor taken his watch.

Cover made his way to the Gallatin Valley, fifty-five miles away, on foot. A party left immediately to bring Bozeman's body in for burial.

The next year the Sioux and Cheyennes forced the army to abandon their forts. After six seasons, the Bozeman Trail had closed.

In 1849 John Bozeman's father had left his wife and five children to join the gold rush to California. His family never heard from him again. In 1862 John left a wife and three small daughters behind when he headed west for riches. His family never heard from him again. The main city in the Gallatin Valley was named Bozeman in his honor.

Suggested reading: Dorothy Johnson, *The Bloody Bozeman* (Missoula: Mountain Press Publ. Co., 1983).

OLD GREENWOOD

Caleb Greenwood was a tough old man. With sons John and Britton, he guided the Stephens-Townsend-Murphy emigrant party to California in 1844. This party was the first to take wagons over the Sierras. Caleb was then eighty-one, but he stood six feet tall, and his thirty years in the fur trade had given him the strength, determination, and brusque manner of getting things done that belied his advanced age.

Caleb had little time for women until he was past sixty. John, his oldest son, was seventeen, and Britton about fifteen that summer of 1844. His five younger children were back with relatives in Missouri, where Caleb's French-Indian wife had just died.

In May, 1845, Caleb went back east to Fort Hall. John Sutter and others had hired him to meet Oregon-bound emigrants and sing the siren song of California. Caleb took John and Britton with him for the summer's employment.

By early August the travelers began arriving from the east. "The trail is easy," Old Greenwood said. "There ain't many Injuns. And it's no problem getting wagons acrost the Seeairies. We done it last year for the fust time. Sutter will meet us with ten men bringing spuds, coffee, and dried beef. Hunting and fishing are better'n Missouri, and the rivers are jumping with salmon. And fer frosting on the cake, Sutter will give every fambly that settles on his grant a thousand acres of free land."

Eight wagons pulled out of the first train. Then came ten, then fifteen. Finally on August 11, with about forty wagons in all, Caleb started for California. A small group of wagons, unwilling to wait for him, had gone on ahead.

As they followed up the Raft River, they saw some old Indian camps. Three days later they saw live Indians as the train crossed into the watershed of the Humboldt River.

At their campground the next evening in Thousand Springs Valley, Caleb told the emigrants about the Indian massacre of eight whites a few years before. The victims' bones still lay on the ground.

They had a friendly visit from Indians on August 27, but these Shoshone guests warned about Paiutes on ahead who would shoot their animals and try to steal. They were crossing the area that Shoshones and Paiutes had fought over for generations. They saw several dead Indians as they approached Battle Mountain.

The emigrants had a moment of panic on September 4, when a cloud of dust looked like Indians attacking. It was just wind. But the next day four oxen were shot by Indians. A group of armed men scoured the bushes for the attackers but found nothing.

Each morning John Greenwood led a small group of scouts out before the rest of the emigrants were ready to travel. They scouted ahead all day and picked out the next campground, where they waited for the others.

By camping time on September 6, the scouts had almost caught up with the small party which had left Fort Hall early. The next morning in Lassen Meadows (south of present Winnemucca), John saw an Indian skulking beside the trail. He whirled quickly and shot the Indian dead.

By the time the main party reached the scene of the shooting, John had ridden on ahead and some of the small, overtaken, wagon party had stayed behind. Caleb thought the Indian had been killed by someone in the small party.

"The man who killed that Indian must die," he declared.

Someone told Caleb that his own son was the killer. Others nodded agreement.

"I guess I better hear the whole damn story, then."

When the witnesses finished talking, Caleb knew that John was the killer. There was no question of self defense.

"I order that the murderer of that Indian be killed," he said, gritting his teeth.

When some of John's friends caught up with him and told him of his father's order, John rode a lot faster.

Old Greenwood led his party on across the Sierras, and they reached Sutter's Fort on September 28. The emigrants' only complaint, other than the difficulty of getting their wagons over the mountains, was the high prices in California.

John Greenwood, accompanied by some of the men in the small party that had gone ahead, reached Sutter's Fort the day before his father got there. Apparently Caleb had cooled off by that time. But for a few days, an eighteen-year-old thought it best to stay away from his 82-year-old father. Besides throwing a scare into his son, Old Greenwood had clearly established that California was directly accessible from the states without having to go through the Oregon country or the Spanish Southwest.

Suggested reading: Charles Kelly and Dale Morgan, *Old Greenwood* (Georgetown, CA.: The Talisman Press, 1965).

A HERO AND A GENTLEMAN

Charles Stanton, thirty-five, had gone broke in a Chicago business. He jumped at the chance to join the Donner-Reed wagon train to California in 1846. A bachelor, he hoped to find fame and fortune in California.

Stanton, only five feet, five inches tall, tried constantly to improve his mind. He taught himself botany and geology. He studied plant life and rock formations along the trail.

After a month's delay in the Wasatch Mountains and a perilous desert crossing south of Great Salt Lake, the emigrants sent Stanton and Bill McCutcheon on ahead.

"Bring back a relief party," the leaders said. "We'll probably need food and help to cross the mountains."

McCutcheon, a six feet, six inch giant from Missouri, traveled with his wife and baby. Normally the emigrants would not have sent an unmarried man like Stanton ahead for fear he might not come back. But they thought McCutcheon would be a good influence on his little partner.

"We'll do our best," Stanton assured the others.

Almost a month later, the emigrants reached Truckee Meadows and began the climb into the Sierras. They met Stanton and two Indians, bringing seven pack mules loaded with food.

"Bill was sick," Stanton said. "He stayed at the fort. Sutter sent two of his Indian vaqueros back with me."

Stanton, serving now as guide in country he had traveled over twice, tried to get the wagons over the mountains. But the oxen were too weak and the snow too deep for the rugged climb. The emigrants built shelters and killed their oxen for food.

In late November Stanton tried again to lead some of the emigrants over the pass and down to Sutter's Fort. This time they left the wagons, and they tried to use the mules as pack animals. The snow lay ten feet deep, with drifts to twenty, and the emigrants were unable to push through it.

"We just can't do it, Charley," they said. "The snow is too deep and the mountains too high."

They gave up and returned to their shelters. Some of the company were close to starvation, and the need to get at least some messengers out was critical.

Stanton had grown up in New York. He and a man from Vermont thought they could make snowshoes. They carved ox-yoke bows into strips and weaved rawhide platforms to stand on. By the end of another long snowstorm — five days in mid-December — they had fourteen pairs.

Besides Stanton and the Indians, seven men, two half-grown boys, and five young women were considered strong enough to try and get out. All but three would have snowshoes. Each person carried a single blanket and rations for six days. Three strips of dried beef, each the size of two fingers, made up a daily ration. They took turns carrying the gun and the axe.

They could still see the shelters at the lake from their first night's camp. Unable to dig down to bare ground, they cut green logs and made a platform for their fire. They crowded around, huddled under their blankets, and spent a miserable night.

They went six miles the next day, camping west of the pass in twelve-foot-deep snow. Going slightly downhill, they went another six miles the third day.

Still above the tree line, the weather was clear and the sun dazzling. Some became snowblind. Stanton suffered the most. He was also the weakest, and he trudged into camp an hour after the others.

The fourth day was like the third. Some began to hallucinate. Mary Graves, sure she saw smoke in the distance, insisted on firing the gun as a signal. Again, Stanton struggled into camp late. On the fifth day they went only four miles.

On the sixth day little Stanton, the bachelor who once was warm and safe in the Sacramento Valley but came back so women and children would have food, could not get to his feet. Starvation and snowblindness had done him in. He sat quietly by the fire, smoking his pipe, as the others moved out. Mary Graves came back and asked if he was coming. He looked up and smiled.

"Yes, Mary, I'm coming soon. You just go on."

Stanton lived as a hero and died a gentleman. His chivalry spared his companions any qualms about deserting him.

Soon the emigrants were eating their dead and killing the Indian vaqueros to eat them, too. But brave Charles Stanton, frozen to death at the fifth night's campsite, would never know.

Suggested reading: George R. Stewart, *Ordeal by Hunger* (Boston: Houghton Mifflin Company, 1960).

DEATH VALLEY HERO

When William Lewis Manly was nine he drove a team and wagon from his native Vermont to Ohio. Later he followed trapping trails in the Northwest Territory (present Michigan and Wisconsin). But his greatest moment came in 1849 when, at age twenty-nine, he became one of California's greatest heroes.

About a hundred wagons of 49ers reached Salt Lake City too late to chance a Sierra crossing. They started southwest on the Old Spanish Trail toward Los Angeles. About a quarter of them, anxious for a short cut, turned west into unfamiliar mountains in southern Nevada. When they reached what we now call Death Valley, it was too late to turn back.

Disorganized, they broke up into small groups, each one struggling to find water for themselves and their oxen. Finally, one group — thirteen adults and four children — sent two of their men on ahead for help. They picked Manly and his friend, John Rogers. The rest would wait by a small spring, hoping for rescue.

They killed an ox and used the hide to make moccasins and backpacks for Manly and Rogers. They divided the meat between the messengers and the ones staying behind. A few handfuls of meat and two spoonfuls of rice and tea was all the food the two men had.

Manly had a rifle and Rogers a shotgun. The ones staying behind included Asabel Bennett and his family, whom Manly had known back in Wisconsin. Mrs. Bennett's words stayed with them as they set out on a cold January day:

"God bless you and help you to bring food to my starving children."

The two men found ice on ridge tops to lick for moisture. They had trouble eating, as their throats were too dry to swallow. Manly wondered if they would starve with meat left in their packs.

They overtook emigrants from other groups — grim, forlorn people, losing hope fast. They passed the body of one man who had already perished. They had only one light blanket. They slept "spoon fashion" to survive the cold nights.

Their first fresh meat was a crow. They devoured the bird. Later that day they shot a hawk. They feasted on hawk stew by a mountain stream in the snow. The food and the first good water they'd tasted in three months made them feel better.

Finally they saw cattle and horses in the distance, a "glimpse of paradise," Manly said, "and tears of joy ran down our faces." By then Manly was so lame he could hardly walk.

They killed the first steer they saw. They hadn't realized how starved they were until they had all the fresh beef they could eat. They both got sick.

They made new moccasins and filled their backpacks with fresh meat, throwing out what they had saved from the starved ox. Vaqueros found them and took them to the Mission San Fernando. They picked up three horses and a mule and did something the emigrants left behind weren't too sure would happen.

Manly and Rogers started back! One of their horses died, but they kept going, knowing full well how terrible was the country they had to go into. They passed the body they had seen before, plus the body of another emigrant.

Worried that some of their group might starve, they took a short cut that the horses could not handle. The plaintive cries from the abandoned animals bothered them. They had to help their mule over some places, but the game little animal carried the food for the survivors they hoped to find.

As they neared the place where they had started, they saw figures moving. Afraid it might be hostile Indians, they watched carefully, their guns ready. Then they heard Bennett call out, "The boys have come back! The boys are here!" It took Bennett a long time before he could talk about the rescue without crying.

Manly and Rogers had been gone twenty-six days and traveled over four hundred miles in one of the most heroic rescues in history.

As Manly led the emigrants out of the valley, someone looked back and said, "Goodbye, Death Valley."

They passed the bodies of the horses they had left behind. They forced their few remaining oxen over precipices by piling up sand for a cushion and pushing the animals over. They reached civilization on March 7, 1850.

Manly worked a while for an emigrant who had escaped with another group. Then he and his little mule went north to look for gold. This California hero will never be forgotten.

Suggested reading: William L. Manly, *Death Valley in '49*, (New York: Wallace Hebberd, 1929).

SKINNED ALIVE

They knew him only as Rebel. He started for California in 1850 with other emigrants from southeastern Missouri. He had no family with him — just one of many single men, walking two thousand miles to a land of new beginning.

Rebel like to talk about how he would kill the first Indian he saw. He talked about it most of the time. He would pat the stock of his rifle and nod, a knowing smile on his face.

The Missourians joined other wagons at Westport and headed northwest. They traveled up the Blue River and then struck overland for Fort Kearney on the Platte. There they hoped to pick up a guide for the long journey to California.

The Missourians paid little attention to Rebel at first. He seemed a big blowhard. But the bragging about killing Indians continued, and the travelers began to talk among themselves about their hate-filled companion.

"Sure seems mad at Injuns."

"Don't rightly know why. Never says much about hisself."

"Got a fambly, yuh reckon?"

"Don't know of airy. He jined up back in the Ozarks."

"Maybe our Missoury Injuns did suthin' bad to him or his people."

"Osages mostly been peaceful."

"Wal he sure talks a lot of killin'."

"Hope it's hot air. Don't need no trouble with Injuns."

"Nor want none, neither."

"That's right smart."

But it was more than hot air. As the wagon train came down Deer Creek toward Fort Kearney, Rebel saw his first Indian.

She was a young mother, who had moved a short distance off the trail to nurse her baby. Before the horrified emigrants could stop him, Rebel grabbed his rifle and shot the woman to death. Then he yelled in fiendish delight, dancing and waving the rifle over his head.

The shocked travelers continued down the trail, looking warily over their shoulders. They shuddered at the sight of the dead mother and her crying baby, its face now smeared with bloodstained milk. They prodded their oxen, hoping the young woman's band would not find her until the wagon train was safely away.

They did not have to wait long. The enraged Indians

caught the train, halting it in its tracks. They demanded the killer.

Rebel studied the older men in the train, now talking together in low tones. Surely, he thought, they wouldn't turn one of their own over to wild savages.

"Ain't no use us gettin' into trouble 'count of him," said one. "I'm fer turnin' him over."

"We're damn lucky they don't jist kill one of our wimmin to get even."

"We could tell him ter make a run fer it," said another. "Might give the pore feller some chanct."

"Wouldn't be no chance 'tall. Why make them mad at us? It warn't none of our doin'."

"I say we give him to the injuns. Had no business killin' that squar. Gits our wimmin in trouble."

"We better grab him 'fore he starts shootin' again."

The men nodded and grunted their agreement. They overpowered Rebel before he could resist, disarmed him, and handed him over to the Indians.

Rebel's furious captors carried him away from the trail and threw him to the ground. Several held his body as Rebel thrashed and twisted. Others drew their knives and began skinning him alive.

The emigrants, now even more horrified, could do nothing. As they moved ahead, Rebel's shrieks and screams died away in the distance, telling them what they were unwilling to turn around and watch.

When the train was five miles east of Fort Kearney, the emigrants went into camp. They met W. F. Drannan and hired him as their guide.

Drannan had just reached the fort after traveling from Bent's Fort with Jim Bridger. Drannan had fought Indians all over the West. He had seen or heard of every imaginable kind of torture inflicted by and against Indians.

"Them Missourians were the most excited people I ever seen," he said. "The Indians' skinning Rebel alive was one of the most terrible experiences on the frontier."

Suggested reading: W. F. Drannan, *Chief of Scouts* (Chicago: Thos. W. Jackson Publ. Co., 1910).

THE KILLING OF OLD JULES

One of the West's wildest towns got its name from a great scoundrel. Frenchman Jules Reni reached the frontier in the 1850s. He built a cabin in the valley of the South Platte River, opposite the mouth of Lodgepole Creek, and began trading with Indians.

When the Leavenworth and Pike's Peak Stage line moved north to avoid hostile Indians, it followed an old road past Jules' place. The company built a station there and hired Jules as its agent.

When the Butterfield Overland Stage took over in the early 1860s, Julesburg, as it was called, became one of its most important stations. The town grew to a dozen buildings, including the station office, Jules' house, a blacksmith shop, a store, a telegraph office, a saloon, and the stables. Liquor was available twenty-four hours a day.

Julesburg became a rendezvous for gamblers, thieves, and renegades of all kinds. They called it the toughest town between the Missouri River and the mountains.

When Ben Holladay took over the stage line, he knew of the town's reputation. Although Holladay, the King of the Plains, was as tough as any man in the West, he changed the name of his station to Overland City. But the fancy name only appeared on company maps. The teamsters, bullwhackers, soldiers, gamblers, and immigrants who stopped there still called it Julesburg.

Holladay foolishly left Jules in charge as agent. Jules robbed his employer blind. Julesburg was in the roughest division on the stage line, and Holladay named his right hand man, Jack Slade, the division superintendent.

Slade, as tough as Holladay, had already killed several men enforcing rules for the stageline's previous owners, Russell, Majors and Waddell.

"Clean up the mess," Holladay told Slade. I don't care how it's done."

Slade found Jules in the saloon.

"You're through," Slade roared. "I'm taking over."

Jules stalled, and Slade threw him out into the street. For the next day or two, Slade examined books, supplies, and company livestock, and he sent more people packing.

But Jack Slade grew careless. Jules caught him in the street and shot him five times with a pistol and once with a full load of buckshot. Slade did put two shots into Jules before he fell.

Jules swaggered up to the fallen man. He rolled Slade over with his foot. "Put him in one of those drygoods boxes and bury the bastard," he growled to one of his henchmen.

Slade stared at his attacker through glassy eyes, but he could speak. "I'll wear your ears on my watch," he sneered, forcing the words through clenched teeth and whitened lips.

Jules laughed and walked away to tend to his own wounds.

The next stage brought a company official to Julesburg. He organized a posse, which captured Jules. They tried to build a gallows, but Jules' gang of hoodlums kept tearing it down. Finally the posse got Jules' head in a noose and jerked him off the ground. Jules nearly strangled before his gang obtained his release on Jules' promise to leave the country.

Holladay spared no expense to provide medical treatment to his horribly-wounded superintendent. Six months in Denver and Saint Louis hospitals put Jack Slade back on his feet, craving revenge. He found Jules at Chauson's Station, twenty-five miles southeast of Fort Laramie. The army also wanted Jules, but Slade found him first.

Slade got the drop on Jules. He dragged him into the station corral and tied him to the fence, his arms outstretched. Slade's actions have since been illustrated in a Charley Russell painting and copied in Hollywood movies.

Slade started shooting in a slow pattern. He shot Jules in one hand and then in the forearm. Then he repeated the pattern in the other hand and arm. Then he moved down to the feet and lower legs. By this time, Jules was begging for the mercy of a quick death, but Slade smiled coldly and continued with his methodical execution.

Slade reloaded his pistols and drew his knife. He advanced to Jules and cut off an ear.

"I told you I'd wear them, didn't I?" He roared with laughter and cut off the other ear.

Then Slade stepped back. Holding his gory trophies in one hand, he took careful aim with the other and ended the torture with a shot through the heart.

Suggested reading: Ellis Lucia, *The Saga of Ben Holladay* (New York: Hastings House, 1959).

FRONTIER JUSTICE

Jesse Stem served the Comanches from his agency on the Clear Fork of the Brazos in Shackelford County, Texas. A hard worker, he discharged his heavy responsibilities well. Danger was his constant companion.

Stem was peacemaker and father confessor not only for the Comanches, but also for Wichitas and Kickapoos in that area. He scolded warriors for stealing horses, trying to persuade them to return the animals to their owners. Often the chiefs merely winked at the offenses.

"We cannot control some of our warriors," they would tell Stem. "You know how it is sometimes with your own young men."

Young braves would often stop at the agency, seeking favors or just a chance to talk. Stem always treated them courteously, using tact and wisdom in meeting their needs.

"Your father in Washington seeks peace with all Comanches," he would say. "He wants to help you in every way possible."

Stem thought the rich, Clear Fork bottom land had sufficient rain to be productive. He spent much spare time developing an experimental farm to show his Indians how to raise food and cash crops. He found a good market for his grain at Fort Belknap.

Stem was more impressed with the farming potential of the Clear Fork bottoms than were the Indians. Finally he resigned as agent to farm for himself.

In 1854, while Stem and a neighboring farmer were riding to Fort Belknap, both men were murdered. The mutilation of their bodies pointed to Indian responsibility, but the local authorities had no clues for several weeks.

Then some Kickapoo Indians, visiting Fort Arbuckle in Indian Territory, told the commanding officer that Kickapoo renegades had committed the murders. The tribe was at peace with the whites, so when the army asked Mosqua, their leader, to come in, the chief came immediately.

"We heard it from a young boy in our tribe," Mosqua said. "He said he'd been down to the Brazos River in Texas with two bad warriors and had seen them kill the two men."

"Well — "

"I tried to arrest them, but they escaped."

Before he left the fort, Mosqua assured the officer the guilty men would be brought to justice.

In March, 1854, several Kickapoos told the army that the killers were Sakokwah and Peatahkak. With this information, Mosqua sent out a party of braves, who captured Peatahkak and started back to the village with him. Although bound with ropes and under heavy guard, the prisoner drew a concealed knife, cut his shackles, and tried to flee. One of the warriors killed him, and they brought his body to Fort Arbuckle.

Mosqua made a public appeal for the arrest or killing of Sakokwah, the other murderer. When Sakokwah made his escape, he had gone to another camp on the Canadian River, where his brother lived. As he rode into the camp, he shouted out loudly:

"I am the man who killed the two white men near the Brazos River. If anybody wishes to take my life, here I am. I am not afraid to die."

No one bothered him as he went on to his brother's lodge, "Here you see me, my brother," he said, "a fugitive from justice. I am hunted down like a wild beast. I am like a wounded deer that cannot escape. I would have gone to the wild Indians, but I feared I would starve before finding them. So I came to you."

The brother fed the killer and then took him for a walk. When they reached the edge of the camp, the brother stepped behind him, raised his axe, and felled him with one blow.

"I have often warned you," the brother said. "Leading a bad life brings trouble and disgrace. You have spurned my advice, broken the law, and brought white displeasure against the whole tribe. They demand reparation for your terrible deed. You have forfeited your life, and it is my painful duty to kill you."

When the brother finished the execution, a council said it was too far to the fort to transport the body. So they cut off the head and carried it to Fort Arbuckle the next day.

Captain Randolph Marcy, leading army explorer and well acquainted with the tribe, said, "Kickapoo justice has a high regard for law and permits no inflexibility in the way its mandates are carried out."

The death of Jesse Stem, faithful friend of Indians, had been properly avenged.

Suggested reading: Carl C. Rister, *Fort Griffin on the Texas Frontier* (Norman: University of Oklahoma Press, 1986).

BIG, NOT-TOO-BRIGHT NORSKY

Viking blood flowed in Jon Rui's veins. He came to the United States from Norway in 1827 with his mother and stepfather, Thom Thomson. They moved into a cabin in Illinois, where Thomson relied on the help of his stepsons, Torstein and ten-year-old Jon, to make a new life in the new world.

Jon worked hard to show his appreciation to Thomson for raising two boys, not his own. Jon would look across the flat Illinois prairies and wistfully remember the tall mountains of his homeland.

"You should see the mountains out west," returning emigrants told him.

"I'll go there some day," Jon vowed.

He worked nights for money to buy his own oxen and wagon. Finally, after fourteen years of hard work, Jon's mother and Thomson thought he had done enough for them.

"Take your oxen and wagon and move on with your own life, Jon," they said. "You deserve that."

Although he was a slow reader and deliberate in thought, Jon Rui never saw a man he could not outwork. "He's a big, not-too-bright Norsky," his friends said, affectionately.

Jon found the Rockies disappointing when he traveled west on the Oregon Trail. He continued on to the Sierras. Now those were mountains worthy of Viking songs!

He settled on Putah Creek in the Sacramento Valley.

Jon enjoyed matching his strength against his beloved mountains. He slept best when curled up in a snowdrift.

"He's part grizzly," his neighbors said.

Jon wrote his family, but letters were few. For half of each year, settlers between Placerville and Carson City got no mail at all. The ninety miles of stage road between the two towns was impassable in winter.

Then Jon answered an advertisement seeking brave men on snowshoes to carry winter mail. Jon knew that the webbed snowshoes he used would not work for long distance travel in winter. He remembered men moving fast on long runners when he was a small boy in Norway. "I need a pair like that to carry the mail," he said.

He carved two oak rails, ten feet long and four inches wide. Together they weighed twenty-five pounds.

When Jon volunteered to carry the mail, he did not think Americans would want a man with a strange, foreign-sounding name. To honor his stepfather, he became John Thompson. Friends began calling the big, not-too-bright Norsky Snowshoe Thompson. He became a living legend, crossing the Sierras in howling blizzards, hurtling down forty-foot-deep snowdrifts with sixty to eighty-pound mailbags on his back.

He never carried a blanket or food that had to be cooked. His night time shelters were holes dug in the snow and lined with evergreen branches.

Once Jon leaped 180 feet. Sixty years would pass before an American broke that record, and then only with modern skis and a carefully groomed approach. But Jon's greatest achievement came in December, 1856, when he found James Sisson in a small cabin near the crest of the mountains. Sisson, injured, had lain in the cabin for twelve days with no way to build a fire. Gangrene had reached both knees.

Thompson brought in firewood, cut the boots off the feverish man, and gave him what food he carried. Then he picked up his heavy bag of Christmas mail and started down the east slope of the Sierras to Genoa, Nevada, where the nearest doctor had his office. He traveled all night.

Doctor Daggett was away on an emergency. But five men went back with Thompson, reaching Sisson's cabin on Christmas Eve. Thompson could barely stand. "You rest, Snowshoe, while we make a sled," someone insisted.

Two feet of snow fell that night. The sled was hard to pull, and they were only half way down when they had to stop for Christmas night. They reached Genoa the next day, but Doctor Daggett said Sisson could not survive the operation without chloroform. The nearest chloroform was in Sacramento!

Thompson had had only two night's sleep since leaving Placerville five days before.

"I'll get what the doctor needs," he said, strapping on his heavy skis.

In a day and a night he reached Placerville. He caught a few hours rest while horsemen brought the chloroform from Sacramento. Then another day and night brought him back to Genoa, where the doctor amputated Sisson's legs.

The patient survived, thanks to a big, not-too-bright Norsky with the blood of Vikings in his veins. Snowshoe Thompson had made five mid-winter crossings of the Sierras in seven days.

Suggested reading: Jack Schaefer, *Heroes Without Glory* (Boston: Houghton Mifflin Co., 1965).

MASSACRE

A wagon train leaving Arkansas for California in 1857 was organized and supplied much better than most. The 140 travelers had forty wagons and over six hundred cattle. Several men were mounted and could scout for game and Indians. Some travelers rode in elegant carriages.

The company had selected an experienced captain. Alexander Fancher, forty-five, was a tall, weather-beaten man. His steady eye and calm speech marked him as a natural leader. He had been to California the year before and knew the route well. His brother John had already settled in Visalia.

"You should see that San Joaquin Valley land," Alexander told neighbors on his return. "Dirt's deep, black and rich. Crumble's nice in your fist and smells like fat hogs, tall corn, and money."

Fancher and his neighbors were prosperous farmers, but like most frontiersmen, they were always interested in moving west. Born in Tennessee, Fancher had already farmed in Illinois and Missouri and in another county in Arkansas. But he was restless, and the West still beckoned.

He and Eliza had eight children, ranging from nineteen-year-old Hampton to five-year-old Kit Carson, named for the famous scout. Fancher's older brother, Hampton, chose not to go, but two of his sons joined their uncle's company.

Other families in the train were even larger than the twelve Fanchers. John Baker, 52-year-old patriarch, headed a close-knit family of over twenty. The Dunlap clan consisted of two brothers with their families, totalling eleven children.

Also on the trail, as the Fancher train approached Utah Territory, were advance elements of the United States Army. President Buchanan, in office just two months, hoped to prevent civil war in the West. He had sent the army to show Mormons, some of whom had over a dozen wives each, that they were still citizens and subject to the nation's laws. Territorial Governor Brigham Young had mobilized all Mormon men into a militia, ready to fight to death for their religious freedom.

Knowing the army was not far behind them, some of the Fancher wagon train taunted the Mormons as they passed through their communities:

"We tuk care of you'uns in Illinois, and we'll do it again. Women slaves haint in God's law."

"The army's on its way. Y'all will see what treason gets."

"Good book says the wages of sin is death."

The train turned south at Salt Lake City and headed for Southern California through a grim and hostile land. When the immigrants reached Cedar City they stopped in a mountain meadow to rest their livestock. They were almost out of Utah. Another hundred miles of desert travel would bring them to low California mountains with an easy passage into the fertile San Joaquin Valley.

Local militia saw the forty excellent wagons and other carriages in the train, the arms, ammunition, and abundant supplies, and particularly the large herd of cattle. They were preparing for war with the United States, and they knew of the insults which these Gentiles had heaped on the saints as they passed through Zion.

What at first was a Mormon decision to defend their homeland turned into the Lord's work of Blood Atonement for the remission of Gentile sins. The faithful had listened all summer to hate-filled sermons about Gentiles. Now the Godless wretches would have their sins washed away in their own blood!

The militia persuaded local Paiute Indians to attack, promising they could have most of the captured cattle. But the immigrants were tougher than they thought. After four days of siege, it was clear the Indians needed help.

In one of the West's most shameful moments, the militia told the immigrants they would help them escape. If the immigrants pretended to surrender, they would be protected and the Indians bought off with a few of the cattle.

The immigrants, without water for four days, were in no position to question the offered help. They followed instructions, and put all their weapons in a wagon. Then they walked out single-file, each man paired with a Mormon. At a pre-arranged signal, each Mormon fired point blank at his prisoner. The Indians, hiding in the brush, fell on the women and children. Only seventeen infants survived.

The bodies of Alexander Fancher, his wife Eliza, their eight children, and two nephews lay surrounded by over a hundred neighbors. Twenty years later, one Mormon was executed for the crime.

Suggested reading: William Wise, *Massacre at Mountain Meadows* (New York: Thomas Y. Crowell Co., 1976).

SAILING TO THE MOUNTAINS

Sam Peppard, Ohio-born millwright, settled in Oskaloosa, Kansas, in 1856 when he was twenty-three. He built a saw and grist mill on Grasshopper River. Two years later gold was discovered on Cherry Creek (near modern Denver) in far western Kansas Territory. After a terrible drouth in 1859 frontiersmen in eastern Kansas began saying, "It's Pike's Peak or Bust."

Sam's friends laughed when he said he'd put canvas on his wagon and sail west.

"Lewis and Clark did it fifty years ago," Sam responded.

"They used canoes and horses. Everybody knows that."

"I saw it in a book," Sam insisted. "They was hauling a boat on wheels. They put the sail up and let the wind help. You'll see."

"Well, there's plenty wind here. Maybe so, it'll work."

With the help of a few friends, Sam had the wagon ready in May, 1860. They towed it a mile south of town to a level stretch of land. Sam climbed aboard and raised the mainsail to a stiff breeze. The craft nearly capsized. But Sam reefed in the mainsail and let out the smaller one. The windwagon went so fast the wheel bearings got hot. Then it climbed a small rise, went airborne about thirty feet, and crashed.

"I guess I have to learn about sailing," Sam said.

The repairs took only a few days. Then Sam and three friends set sail for the Rockies. Their provisions, camping outfit, and guns weighed four hundred pounds. They tacked northwest to the Oregon Trail near the Little Blue River. They followed the trail to Fort Kearney and on west along the South Platte River. They found more room to maneuver by traveling away from the river, parallel to the trail ruts.

"Our best time was two miles in four minutes," Sam remembered. "If we went faster, the bearings heated up. One day we passed 625 wagons."

But while thirty knots was a good cruising speed on the plains and the wind always blew, it didn't always blow the right direction. It came from a favorable direction only nine days of the four weeks they were on the trail.

A correspondent for *Leslie's Illustrated Magazine* described the windwagon's travel past Fort Kearney:

"The ship hove in sight with a fresh breeze from east-northeast, running down for the fort under full sail. Two masts, somewhat raked, carry large square sails. A large coach lamp in front allows night travel when the wind is favorable; and it is steered by a helm attached to the fore wheels. Getting clear of the fort, she again caught the breeze, and went off at a dashing rate towards Pike's Peak. She stampeded all the animals on the road, scattering the horses and mules of the old fashioned travelers."

About fifty miles north-northeast of Denver the crew saw a dust devil approaching. They had met several on their journey and knew to lower the sail until the whirlwind was past. This time, however, a rope caught in a pulley. In his haste, Peppard jerked too hard, and the rope broke. With no way to lower the sail, the whirlwind carried the wagon about twenty feet into the air. It came down on the hind wheels, which broke under the weight.

The crash ended their five hundred mile journey. Leaving the wreck behind, Peppard and his crew joined a slow but steady baggage train for the rest of the trip.

Suggested reading: David Dary, *True Tales of the Old-Time Plains* (New York: Crown Publishers, 1979).

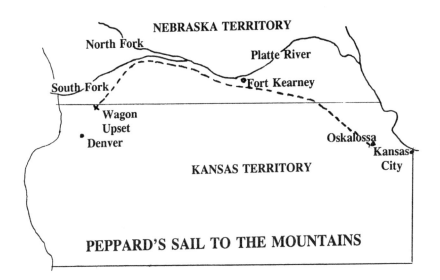

PEPPARD'S SAIL TO THE MOUNTAINS

SOCK RACE

John Applegate, Ralph Rosier, and Lafayette "Bolly" Bolwinkle tended the Mountain Springs Station in eastern Nevada in the early 1860s. The Pony Express, the mule mail, and westward-traveling emigrants kept them busy.

Station keeping was a tough job. The Indians killed far more station keepers than they did Pony Express riders.

One morning Applegate and Rosier got up at daylight to be ready for the west-bound Pony Express rider coming from Butte Station. Rosier went down to the spring for water while Applegate started the fire for breakfast. Bolly snuggled down in his blankets for forty more winks.

A shot rang out, and Applegate ran to the door to look out. Bolly raised up in his blankets.

"What the hell was that?" Bolly asked.

"They got Rosie," Applegate yelled. "He's only ten rods from the door. Maybe I can drag him in."

A second shot rang out, and Applegate slumped to the floor, shot through the groin. Bolly stumbled out of his bunk, grabbing for his clothes.

Si McCandless kept a small trading store across the road, where he lived with his Gosiute woman. When he heard the shots, he ran to the station. The attacking Indians, considering McCandless a relative, held their fire.

"Barricade the door with them sacks of grain," McCandless shouted as he ran in.

McCandless and Bolly struggled with the sacks as they watched Applegate, bleeding on the floor.

"You gonna be alright, John?" McCandless asked. He knew, from running past the body, that Rosier was already dead.

"Don't try to save me, boys," Applegate groaned. "I'm a goner. See if you can save yourselves."

"Not by a damn sight," Bolly shouted. "We'll stay right with you, John."

As Si and Bolly barricaded the door, Applegate dragged himself to the window and pulled up to look out.

"Gimme a gun, quick," Applegate called out.

Thinking their companion had seen an Indian target, the others handed Applegate a revolver.

"Goodbye, boys, now save yourselves," Applegate muttered through clenched teeth. Before the other two could stop him, Applegate shot himself through the head.

Si and Bolly were stunned for a moment. Then Si said, "Bolly, we gotta beat it fer Butte Station."

"But it's twelve miles. The devils will get us, sure, if we make a run for it."

"No they won't if you do what I tell you. They're not after me, 'count of my woman. They coulda got me if they wanted to. We can out run 'em. If you stay right in front of me, they won't shoot for fear of hitting me."

"Might as well try it," Bolly said. "Ain't much use in staying here to be killed slow like."

Bolly was still in his stocking feet. In all the excitement, he'd forgotten to put boots on. He and McCandless shoved some grain sacks aside, flung open the door, and bolted out.

The yelling Indians chased after them, but McCandless, a good athlete, kept Bolly directly in front of him. When Bolly faltered, McCandless put his hands under the other man's arms and helped him along.

Finally, the Indians gave up the chase and returned to the station to complete their looting and to scalp their victims. McCandless and Bolly, moving as fast as possible with Bolly's bleeding feet, could hear the savage yells receding in the distance.

After twelve miles of bleeding and pain, Bolly staggered into Butte Station on bruised and swollen feet. McCandless had to help him stand upright.

As soon as the runners gasped out the bad news, Billy Fisher jumped on a horse and struck out for Egan Canyon to warn the stations to the east. He picked Wash Perkins up at Shell Creek and they rode together to Simpson's Springs, where they found Major Howard Egan, superintendent of that part of the Pony Express.

Egan and Perkins rode back west to begin the work of re-opening Mountain Springs and other stations closed by the Indian attacks. Several months passed before Lafayette Bolwinkle could walk without pain. He never again ran a race in his stocking feet.

Suggested reading: Howard R. Driggs, *The Pony Express Goes Through* (New York: J. P. Lippincott Co., 1963).

A PICTURESQUE AND DARING MAN

Pierre Garreau's ancestry puzzled even him. His Mandan mother married French trader Antoine Garreau, who lived with the Mandan, Hidatsa, and Arikara tribes. Pierre considered Antoine his father, although the man died before Pierre had many memories. Frederick Girard, a French-Indian trader who knew Pierre well, said Garreau's mother married the Frenchman shortly after her Mandan husband died, and that Pierre was a full blood Mandan.

Garreau's muscular body gave no clue to the puzzle. At five feet, ten with a forty-six-inch chest, he weighed over two hundred pounds. He could lift a three hundred pound keg of trade goods. But the facial features of Pierre, without doubt one of the most picturesque and daring men in the fur trade, strongly suggested he was not a full blood Indian.

Pierre spoke French in addition to the languages of the three tribes he lived with. He also spoke Sioux and English, although not well. He could not read or write. Fur traders in the upper Missouri River country of present North Dakota found his services as interpreter invaluable. His daring and initiative in fighting Sioux and Assiniboines made him a legend.

Seventeen Assiniboines once ambushed Garreau while he hunted near Dog Den Butte with a French employee of Fort Clark. After the attackers killed the Frenchman, Garreau stood up, threw his rifle to the ground, and shouted, "I don't know who you are, but I am Long Hair. Come on and get me. I won't be shot down like a dog by my own campfire."

The enemy, elated at capturing such an illustrious hunter, started to bind his arms. Gareau said he would go without being bound like an animal. They marched him on foot between two mounted warriors until they stopped for a smoke. They sat down in a circle on the prairie and started passing the pipe. They put Garreau in the center of the circle for safe-keeping. When the pipe reached the chief, the captive leaped to his feet and grabbed the pipe, saying "I smoke first. I am the chief here."

Before the startled chief could react, Garreau grabbed him with a paralyzing grip in his side and drew his own gun from inside his shirt. Then he turned to the stunned warriors, challenging them to shoot. He said he was ready to die; he just wanted to take a brave man with him.

The Assiniboines backed down. Garreau ordered the

warriors away on foot, saying he would release the chief when they were out of sight. He let the chief have a horse. He drove the other sixteen captured horses back to Fort Clark.

On Christmas day, 1863, twenty Sioux attacked the trading post at Fort Berthold. Garreau and four other men were the only defenders. An attacker approached a porthole with a burning stick. Garreau, anticipating the move, waited with a lariat in the bastion above the port. He roped the attacker and tried to pull him up into the bastion through an opening in the overhang. The Sioux turned his body sideways so it could not be pulled through. Garreau held the enemy there while he cut his throat and scalped him. Then he challenged the rest of the attackers to come on for the same treatment. The terror-stricken Sioux left, and the fort was saved. The dead warrior's bloodstains marked the fort palisade for many years.

In 1866 Garreau again saved Fort Berthold from the Sioux. This time a hundred warriors rode up, dismounted, and formed a circle outside the gate to dance themselves into a pre-attack frenzy. Garreau burst out of his room wearing a fancy blue shirt with a red sash circling his waist, and a bright red handkerchief around his head. He held two long knives in his hands. He ordered the five-man garrison, astonished at his appearance, to fling the gate open.

With a loud war-whoop Garreau jumped into the center of the Sioux circle. He boasted of killing a brother of one of the Sioux and of capturing the Assiniboine chief. "I want one of you to take one of these knives and fight me," he shouted. "We'll see who is brave."

Garreau strutted around the circle, offering the knife to each Sioux. None would accept. The cowed attackers slunk out of sight as Garreau's taunts about being old women — fit only for camp drudgery — followed them.

In 1881 Garreau, well into his eighties, died a tragic death. Old, infirm, and without a family, he lived alone in a cabin just outside Fort Berthold. The cabin caught fire one night, and the old man was trapped inside. They found his body just inside the door, where he had suffocated from smoke.

Suggested reading: Ethel Collins, "Pioneer Experiences of Horatio H. Larned," in *Collections, North Dakota Historical Society, v. 7* (1925).

THE DEATH OF HENRY GEERY

In spring 1863 the gold camp at Bannack in present Montana was crowded. Jim Stuart, a veteran of the California gold rush, persuaded several men to join him prospecting along the Yellowstone River. Thirteen left with Stuart on April 9. The rest, under Tom Cover and Bill Fairweather, would catch up later.

As Stuart's party crossed the beautiful valley of the Madison, Henry Geery and Richard McCafferty found a promising strike. They kept quiet, afraid that disclosure at that time would break up the party.

"We'll check it out on the way back," they told each other.

The party crossed the Gallatin River and went down the Shields to the Yellowstone. They met a band of Bannock Indians returning from a raid on the Flatheads. Winnemucca, famous chief of the Northern Paiutes, was traveling with them. Wet Flathead scalps hung from their belts.

The party ran into Crow Indians, who tried to steal everything in sight and got much of it. When they reached the Yellowstone, Sam Hauser tried to swim it. He had to give up in the frigid water.

On May 4 they reached the mouth of the Big Horn. Geery almost drowned trying to swim there. The whirlpools at the confluence of the Yellowstone and Big Horn were too much for him.

Jim Stuart noted, "Geery is a splendid swimmer, and that is all that saved his life, for a common swimmer would have been drowned."

After prospecting a while they turned south up the Big Horn River. An Indian attack on May 13 killed two of the party. Others, including Geery, were wounded. He had an arrow in the shoulder. Their tents were riddled. After the battle ended, the men picked up forty-eight arrows from their position. They decided to strike south toward the Emigrant Trail, rather than remain in such hostile Indian country.

Ephriam Bostwick had been wounded five times. Conscious, but in terrible agony, he could not travel. "Just give me a cocked revolver," he muttered between pain-racked lips. "I'll get even with the red devils when they reach me."

Someone handed him a weapon. A few minutes later, the party was horror-stricken as he blew out his brains.

Deep snow slowed the men down. They only made

twenty miles in the first day of their escape attempt. The next day they traveled five miles before stopping for breakfast. They knew the enemy was hovering about, waiting to attack. At that stop Geery, while pulling his rifle from his blankets, accidentally shot himself.

Everyone could see it was a bad wound, and Geery would no longer be able to keep up. "I'm a goner," Geery said. "The rest of you just keep on. Leave me here." He clutched his pistol tightly.

No one knew what to say. Jim Stuart and a few others said something about not abandoning their brave friend, but all could see that his life was fast ebbing away. There was no way to comfort him, so little was said. Stuart, feeling responsible for the others in their peril and knowing that hostile Indians were near, tried to talk Geery out of his decision. But he knew the tragedy that awaited if they did not keep going. Geery, still as brave as ever, solved the problem.

"Remember," he said, "I'm not committing suicide. I'm just taking away a few hours so you men won't sacrifice your lives trying to defend what little is left of mine." He pointed the pistol at his chest.

Stuart pleaded once more to reconsider. Geery was adamant.

"Well, if you're going to do it," Stuart said, "don't do it in the chest. It'll only prolong the agony. Do it in the head."

Geery nodded and smiled. He moved the pistol. "Thanks, Jim. May God bless you all."

When Geery pulled the trigger, the weapon misfired. He looked puzzled. "That never happened before," he said. Rejecting the argument of some that the misfire was a sign that he was doing the wrong thing, Geery recocked the pistol. This time it worked.

Stuart's party reached Bannack on June 20. There they learned that the Cover-Fairweather party that was supposed to join them on the Yellowstone had turned back because of Indian hostility. About four weeks before, that party had discovered gold at Alder Gulch.

Henry Geery's swimming friend, Sam Hauser, would later be governor of Montana. Geery's bones still lie somewhere in the beautiful valley west of the Big Horn Mountains.

Suggested reading: Dan L. Thrapp, *Vengeance: The Tom Cover Saga* (El Segundo: Upton & Sons, 1989).

RANSOM NEGOTIATIONS

Britt Johnson, a free black man, worked on Elizabeth Fitzpatrick's ranch in Texas during the Civil War. The ranch, on Elm Creek just above its junction with the Brazos, was practically unguarded. Elizabeth was between husbands, and most younger Texans had gone east to fight. With the constant threat of Indian attack, Britt and his wife, Mary, worried about their four young children.

On October 13, 1864, seven hundred Comanches and Kiowas crossed the Brazos and raided up Elm Creek, the largest Indian raid in Texas during the Civil War. No men were present to defend the Fitzpatrick ranch. Britt had gone to a trading post at Weatherford for supplies.

When the raiders reached the ranch, Elizabeth herded the women and children into the house. She yelled at the Indians to leave her horses alone. Mary Johnson armed herself with a rifle and fired at the intruders. The Indians killed young Jimmy Johnson and Elizabeth's grown daughter. They captured Mary, two Johnson daughters, Elizabeth, her twelve-year-old son, and her two granddaughters. After raiding other ranches, the warriors rode north to their own territory in present Oklahoma. In addition to taking seven captives, they had killed eleven persons.

A heartsick Britt returned to find Mary and his two daughters gone, and Jimmy killed. He did have some good news. One daughter, Sallie, had been at a neighbor's to try on a dress, and she was unhurt.

In April, 1865, Britt set out to find his family. He wanted to buy them back from their Indian captors, along with the other captives. Sixty miles north of the settlements, he rode up on an Indian guarding a herd of horses. Talking in Spanish, the Indian said the Kiowas had Britt's family and he thought the Comanches had all the whites. The Indian said he would ride with Britt if he would wait until other Indians brought more horses. In a few days the horses arrived. Britt recognized them as belonging to Elm Creek ranches, but he kept quiet about that.

Britt and his Indian companion found Elizabeth Fitzpatrick with Comanches on the Canadian River. She told him to spare no expense in his ransom effort. He rode on to the Kiowas and found Mary and the girls.

Britt had to make four trips to the Kiowas before he got his family back later that fall. The Indians insisted that he negotiate separately for each person. Mary had had a baby during her captivity, and the Kiowas even insisted that Britt pay ransom for that child. Each time Britt reached a satisfactory price and brought the horses, corn, and other goods from the settlements, the Kiowas backed out, saying that other chiefs had not agreed. Finally he got them all together and reached a binding agreement. The Kiowas even provided horses for the captives to ride home.

A Comanche chief, friendly to Britt, had warned him to travel day and night so the Kiowas could not overtake them and re-capture the ransomed captives. The Comanches even provided two men to assist Britt. They rode with him until they were out of Kiowa country. As a parting shot, the Kiowas promised Britt they would kill him if they ever saw him again.

After his long negotiations, Britt had recovered all the captives except one of Elizabeth Fitzpatrick's granddaughters and Elizabeth's young son. The granddaughter had been adopted by a childless Kiowa couple who hid her from Britt, saying they knew nothing about her. The son had been killed by Indians when he got sick the day after the raid and couldn't keep up.

The Kiowas kept their promise to Britt about killing him on sight. In 1871 he was returning from Fort Richardson, where he had hired three black ex-soldiers to help him on the ranch. When the Kiowas attacked, the four men killed their horses and forted up behind the bodies as a breastworks. The piles of cartridge casings told how dearly they had sold their lives.

The Indians scalped all four men, but soon discarded their trophies. The short, kinky hair made the scalps unattractive to the Kiowas. They did rip the bodies open, and they placed Britt's dead dog in his.

Britt and Mary had had two more children after he ransomed her from the Kiowas. The courageous frontiersman left a grieving wife and six children. He was remembered fondly as one of the heroes of northwest Texas.

Suggested reading: Mildred Mayhall, *Indian Wars of Texas* (Waco: Texian Press, 1965).

THE MAIL MUST GO THROUGH

Army posts along the Upper Missouri were not connected by telegraph. Carrying dispatches in winter was usually left to hired civilians, frontiersmen familiar with the land who could survive blizzards and avoid hostile Indians. The 1867-1868 winter was so severe and the Sioux so warlike that even large bonuses to the regular mail carriers could not persuade them to travel above Fort Stevenson, a post about fifty miles north of present Bismarck, North Dakota.

The post commander at Fort Buford, one hundred twenty-five miles further upriver, was determined to keep communication open between his fort and Forts Berthold and Stevenson. Finally Joseph L'Espagnol, called Joe the Spaniard although he was Mexican, agreed to make one round trip to Fort Stevenson for two hundred dollars.

The army fitted him out with a dog travois. They selected the dog, ran shafts from his shoulders to the ground behind, and suspended a platform between the shafts to carry mail and food for both man and animal. Joe and the dog left Fort Buford on February 13, 1868.

Joe had no trouble until he was about two-thirds of the way to Fort Berthold. He avoided three camps of Santee Sioux by leaving the Missouri River and traveling around ravines so the Indians could not see him. This was the tribe that attacked and massacred Minnesota settlers six years before.

Knowing that only friendly Hidatsa Indians should be between him and Fort Berthold, Joe decided to spend the next night in an abandoned log cabin. Thirteen Sioux out hunting saw chimney smoke from Joe's breakfast fire the next day. Three came to the door and demanded to know to whom the packet on the travois belonged.

"It's mail for civilians," Joe replied.

"You lie. It's the soldiers' mail on the Yellowstone."

Thinking he faced only three, Joe put his hand on his revolver. They jumped him, tore the gun from his hand, beat him, and threw him to the ground. When Joe reached for his knife, they wrenched it away, cutting Joe's hands. More beatings followed as the rest of the Indians ran into the cabin. Finally, one Indian knocked Joe out with a gun-butt blow to the back of the head.

Joe regained consciousness to find the Indians amusing themselves by pulling out his beard and mustache, one hair at a time. He was soaked in blood, and his head throbbed in pain. His head, face, and one hand were torn and bleeding. The Indians forced their half-dead victim to cook their breakfast, beating him when he faltered. They killed his dog, chopped up the travois, threw the mail into the fire, and removed all Joe's clothing except a shirt and trousers.

As the Indians gathered together his gun, blanket, shoes and overcoat, Joe begged them to kill him rather than leave him there to die. One Indian notched an arrow, but another said, "Let him die slow."

Although barefooted, bare-headed, and weak, Joe tried to reach Fort Berthold in the deep snow. He walked the rest of the day, all night, and all the next day. The wind increased, and a blizzard filled the air with snow until Joe couldn't see. Finally, when all strength was gone, he lay down in the snow to die.

A party of Hidatsas found him, barely alive. In his confusion he had gone upriver, instead of down. The Indians dressed his wounds, wrapped him in a buffalo robe and got him on a horse. They kept him two days in their camp and then carried him to Fort Berthold. He obtained clothing and made his way on to Fort Stevenson, arriving March 6.

General Philippe de Tobriand, commander at Stevenson, was astonished that Joe insisted on leaving the next day to return to Fort Buford.

"I hired out for $200," Joe said, "and I'll get it or leave my bones on the trail."

De Tobriand did understand Joe's desire for vengeance. Joe remembered one of his attackers by a scar on his eye. The general wrote in the post records that he thought that man was as good as dead.

De Tobriand would not allow such a gallant man to leave on foot. He fitted him out with a blanket and provisions and gave him a horse to ride. Joe the Spaniard left Fort Stevenson on March 7 with his dispatches and correspondence for Fort Buford. Then history closes its door on a brave man. Hopefully he got through.

Suggested reading: Philippe de Tobriand, *Army Life in Dakota* (Chicago, The Lakeside Press, 1941).

DUEL ON THE MAIL ROUTE

Luther Kelly of Geneva, New York, was only fifteen when he enlisted in the 10th Infantry. When the Civil War ended a few months later, the army sent him to Dakota Territory to serve out his three-year hitch. Discharged at eighteen, he headed on west for adventure.

As he crossed the Mouse River loop he met Sitting Bull and his Hunkpapa Sioux. When he reached Fort Buford in January, 1869, he learned that the two men hired to carry mail to Fort Stevenson and back had failed to show up. The army asked for volunteers.

"I need the work," Kelly said. "I'll go."

"It's suicide for one man alone," said men at the fort.

"If he's game the job's his," an army officer said.

Kelly headed downstream with the mail. He passed through Fort Berthold and the stockade of Red Mike Welsh without incident. When he reached Fort Stevenson, the fort commander, Colonel de Trobriand, greeted him.

"Stay a few days, young man," De Trobriand said. "When the mail gets here from forts Totten and Abercrombie, you can head back to Buford."

Kelly impressed De Trobriand. "He's a tall, vigorous, fine lad, with a very intelligent and intrepid air," the colonel wrote.

Kelly merely remembered De Trobriand as a "portly man with a pleasant face."

The mail from the east came in, and Kelly started back to Fort Buford on February 3. He reached Mike's stockade late that night. Bloody Knife and some Arikaras were there.

"Come hunt with us sometime," Bloody Knife said. "We heard your rifle shoots true."

About five miles down the trail the next morning, Kelly was riding through some cottonwoods when he saw two Sioux approaching. Kelly was not alarmed when they dismounted, as Sioux often did that to chat with friends. Nevertheless, he pulled his Henry rifle from its scabbard and slowed his horse to a walk.

When Kelly was about thirty yards away, the Indians suddenly fired, one with a shotgun, the other with a bow. Then the Indian with the bow ran one way to hide behind a large cottonwood. The one with the gun ran the other way into heavy brush.

Kelly jumped from his horse and fired at the Indian in

the brush. The man dropped out of sight, but Kelly was not sure he had hit him. He feared it might be a ruse to make him careless. By now, Kelly was between the two Indians.

All three horses ran away. Kelly feared that his had been hit in the shotgun blast. Now Kelly found himself in a duel with the Indian who had the bow.

From time to time the Indian shot an arrow. Between shots, he kept pushing part of his robe out from the tree to entice Kelly into shooting. Kelly knew the Indian was trying to run him out of ammunition. He still worried about the other man who had disappeared into the brush.

An arrow struck Kelly's knee but he could still stand. Once during the duel, Kelly shouted, "Who are you?" The Indian replied, "Oglala me," but would say no more. Kelly feared the Indians might be scouts for a war or hunting party who would hear the shooting and come to investigate.

But Kelly kept cool. Finally, he got a clear shot and broke the arm of the Indian behind the tree. The Indian then rushed toward him, trying to notch an arrow as he ran. Kelly dropped him with a well-placed shot.

Now Kelly turned and ran back to Red Mike's stockade as fast as he could. He expected to see mounted Indians in pursuit at any time.

Shortly after Kelly reached the stockade, Bloody Knife and his Arikaras rode in. They had heard the shooting from where they were hunting. When they heard Kelly's story, they jumped on their horses and galloped away. They were back in an hour, singing and waving two fresh Sioux scalps.

After Kelly treated his wounded knee, he and Mike rode to the scene of the duel. There they found the two scalped Indians. Kelly collected a nice double-barreled shotgun — one barrel still loaded — and a bow, arrows, robes, moccasins, and other trophies.

Eight years later, serving as chief scout for Nelson Miles, Kelly would miss the Little Bighorn Battle where Sitting Bull's warriors fought the 7th Cavalry, and Bloody Knife, Custer's favorite scout, was killed. By then, though, the New Yorker was famous, himself, as Yellowstone Kelly, intrepid frontiersman of the north who had fought a celebrated duel on the mail route.

Suggested reading: M. M. Quaife, ed. *The Memoirs of Luther S. Kelly* (Lincoln: University of Nebraska, 1973.)

YELLOWSTONE KELLY

Montana Historical Society, Helena

JERRY POTTS

Glenbow Archives, Calgary, Alberta

LONG ON COURAGE, SHORT ON WORDS

When the first Canadian Mounties rode west in 1874 to drive the whiskey traders from Fort Whoop-Up, they got lost. They went down to Fort Benton, Montana Territory, looking for a guide. Fortunately for the later development of the dominion, they found a small, weasel-eyed, bandy-legged half-blood, aged thirty-four, named Jerry Potts.

Two things about Canada's development were strikingly different from the United States: they had practically no trouble with their natives, and an incredibly small number of police kept order in a gigantic land. Jerry Potts, a great frontiersman, deserves much of the credit.

The son of a Scot father, Andrew Potts who managed a fur post, and a Piegan mother, Crooked Back, Jerry was renowned for courage and stamina. The Mounties hired him to guide them to Whoop-Up. The whiskey traders were gone and the Mounties tried unsuccessfully to buy the fort. Then Jerry led them to an excellent site a couple of rivers further west. There they built Fort MacLeod, their first outpost, and began a twenty-three year employment of Jerry as guide and interpreter.

When Jerry was a year old, a Canadian Blackfoot Indian murdered his father. When he was seventeen, Jerry tracked the man down, engaged him in a furious fight which scarred Jerry for life, and killed him. The man's relatives, respecting Jerry's courage, let him go home. Jerry became that rare half-blood who earned high respect from both races.

In late 1870 Jerry fought in the last great Indian battle in Canada. The Blackfoot Confederacy (Blackfoots, Bloods, and Piegans) fought the Cree on the plains near present Lethbridge, Alberta. It began with a Cree slaughter of a camp of undefended Piegan women and children. After a long and bloody battle, the Cree warriors fled the field. Jerry, a veteran of skirmishes with Sioux and Crow, was the hero. He had nineteen Cree scalps, an arrow through his body, and a shotgun pellet embedded below his left ear. Jerry, proud of the pellet, treated it as a good-luck charm.

One time Jerry was traveling with two others in the Montana foothills when a big band of Sioux Indians attacked. The three men rode as fast as they could to a deserted log cabin, where they turned their horses loose and ran inside to barricade themselves. After a furious battle in which eight or ten Sioux fell, the rest withdrew for a conference. Jerry knew what was coming. When darkness fell, the cabin would be set afire, and the Sioux would gather three scalps.

But Jerry slipped away as it grew dark, crawled to the rear of the Sioux camp, and stole three horses. He led them back to the cabin, unseen, and got his companions. All three escaped.

Jerry had similar exploits with the Mounties, and they came to realize that he was as daring as the bravest one of them.

In March, 1875, Jerry led four Mounties on a 300-mile journey to Helena, Montana. As they neared the border a fierce blizzard struck. They had packhorses and supplies, but no tent. Jerry showed them how to dig holes in a riverbank, where they crouched for thirty-six hours, undoubtedly saving some lives.

In 1879 the first Mountie was killed by an Indian. The victim, Marmaduke Grayburn, was nineteen and had been in the force less than six months. Jerry led the search party that found Grayburn's body in the snow-covered hills. He found clues and helped arrest the killer.

Jerry Potts may have been the most laconic interpreter in history. At the first formal meeting between the Mounties and the Blackfoot Conspiracy, he was asked to interpret the lengthy speech of a chief.

He waited until the end, shrugged his shoulders, and said, "Dey damn glad you're here."

When the Governor-General met another group years later, one of the main speakers — appropriately named Loud Voice — harangued him at great length. When the speaker finished, all fair-skinned heads turned to Jerry.

"He wants grub," Jerry said.

In early 1896 the lead pellet worked its way out of Jerry's head. The loss of his good-luck charm bothered him. Later that year he died from throat cancer. The Mounties buried him at Fort MacLeod with full military honors.

Samuel B. Steele, who would go on to become a knight and an army general after a distinguished career in the Mounted Police, said:

"As a scout and guide I have never met his equal, in either the northwest or the states to the south."

Suggested reading: Grant MacEwan, *Fifty Mighty Men* (Saskatoon: Western Producer Prairie Books, 1982).

RANGERS TO THEIR STATIONS

Indian depredations in the early 1870s caused Texas to form a six-company Ranger battalion for frontier defense. Battalion commander John Jones was a Civil War veteran. Most of his captains had fought Indians, but many of the rangers were teen-aged boys looking for excitement.

The battalion had to defend four hundred miles of frontier. Jones rode the length of that frontier, placing the locally-raised companies in the best defensive positions. He started with Captain C. R. Perry's company, raised in Blanco County. He moved them northwest to Menard County.

Taking six men from Perry's company as an escort, Jones rode south to position Captain Caldwell's company, the most southern of the six. Adding six of Caldwell's men to his escort, Jones rode back north to position Captain Malthy. Picking up six more men, he positioned Captain Waller. Then, with twenty-four in his escort, he rode on north to reach Captain Stevens. When they reached Stevens' camp on July 11, 1874, most of the company was out looking for Indians. The next morning, scouts came in.

"We found the trail of a bunch of hostiles leading right toward the settlements," they said.

Jones detailed some of Stevens' company and some of his escort to stay and guard the camp. He took the rest, about twenty-five men, to follow the trail.

"None of the men, other than the major, had ever been under fire," wrote Ed Carnal, one of Jones' patrol. "When we caught up with the Indians, a great deal of promiscuous shooting ensued."

Carnal had a thrilling one-mile ride, pursued by Indians shooting at every jump and yelling like demons. "I kept my head tight against my horse's neck, one hand gripping the mane and the other my revolver. To say I was scared would be putting it mildly."

The Indians circled and continued to attack as the embattled rangers, held in formation by their cool major, moved steadily into a ravine. The rangers dismounted and scrambled into a defensive position, keeping their horses tied nearby. They found they had to rely on their revolvers, as their single-shot carbines were too slow.

When the first ranger was hit, three men volunteered to ride out and bring him in. A courier slipped out to get help from black cavalry troops stationed at Fort Richardson.

Late in the afternoon of that long, hot day, two volunteers rode a half mile to a creek for water. About twenty-five Indians tried to cut them off.

One of the volunteers started back toward the ravine but never made it. The other turned his horse loose and jumped in the creek. He swam and waded, ducking under whenever the Indians got close. After traveling several miles, he found another ranger who had been wounded and cut off earlier in the battle. The two of them eventually reached a ranch twelve miles away.

Back at the ravine, the Indians continued their attack.

"The Indian bullets cut the limbs above us like a mowing machine," Carnal said.

The Indians withdrew at sundown. By then only two or three of the rangers' horses were still alive. They caught some loose Indian horses and loaded up their dead and wounded and their saddles and equipment. Then they set out on foot, leading the horses.

"We were a forlorn and desperate looking crew," Carnal said, "as we filed silently through the timber."

Near dawn they reached the same ranch the other two rangers had found. Those rangers had buried a dead comrade and had welcomed a cavalry patrol from Fort Richardson.

After daylight Major Jones led his survivors and the cavalry patrol back to the battlefield. He wanted to find the Indians' trail and set the cavalry on it.

They did find the ranger who had been shot near the creek. His head had been cut off and the rest of his body mutilated. They dug a grave with bowie knives and drinking cups and buried what was left of their friend.

The Indians had so mixed up their tracks that no exit trail could be found, so the cavalry troopers returned to their fort.

"Captain Stevens," Jones said, "I think your company is already in a good place to protect the settlements from Indians."

Jones picked up those of his escort who had been left at the camp, and they went on to Jacksboro, where they obtained new horses. Then they resumed their march north to position Captain Ikard's company on the Pease River, the last of the six ranger companies on the line of defense.

Suggested reading: Ed Carnal, "Reminiscences of a Texas Ranger," in *Frontier Times* (Bandera, Texas: December, 1923).

OWL HOOTS IN THE NIGHT

Most western frontiersmen believed in the death bird, a mysterious bird which flew at night to warn of danger, most often protecting peace officers, women and children. The bird, never seen in daylight, was supposed to resemble an owl. It had long, slender wings, black as midnight, with a large head and beak.

Texas Ranger Isaac Motes first heard the bird's cry in 1871, when he and four other rangers were stationed at Albany in present Shackelford County. Most of their company was stationed in Fort Worth, over a hundred miles away.

When the Albany rangers learned that Comanches were expected to raid down from Indian Territory, they dispatched Indian Jim, a friendly scout, to ride their fastest horse to Fort Worth for help. Indian Jim should have been back in three days, but he did not return when expected.

The next day, Motes started for Fort Worth to speed up the other rangers. He rode along the high ground to avoid Indian ambush. About half way to Fort Worth, his horse became lame. Darkness was coming on, and he decided to camp in the timber along the Clear Fork of the Brazos.

Once he saw what looked like an Indian's head, bobbing up and down in some distant hills. He thought hostile Indians were in those hills, but he didn't want to find out by himself.

He felt secure camping away from the river in a narrow valley. He hid his horse and his camp under the drooping limbs and overhanging vines of a heavy growth of post oaks.

After rubbing his horse's leg, Motes fixed his own bed at the base of a large tree and lay down, his rifle and revolver at his side. The night was warm, and he heard distant thunder as he fell asleep.

About midnight he woke up to more thunder and lightning. He felt uneasy, wondering if something beside the thunder had awakened him. Then he heard an owl hoot about a hundred yards to the west. He paid no attention at first, but by the third time, the hoot sounded unnatural.

Motes knew that Indians signalled each other with owl hoots as they crept up on their prey. With his ears straining into the moonless darkness, he heard the hoot again, this time to the east. Certain now that he was surrounded, Motes' eyes searched intensely each time the lightning flashed.

Then he heard the scream of the death bird. From the drawn-out, wailing sound, it seemed to have been in the tree overhead and to have flown away to another tree. Then a bolt of lightning blinded the whole river bottom, and Motes expected a shower of arrows from concealed Indians.

When darkness returned, he hastily fixed his saddle and bedroll to look like a sleeping man. With his pistol in his belt and clutching his rifle closely, he rolled away, following the downslope toward the river. Whenever lightning flashed, he stopped and froze still until it was again dark. When he got a hundred feet away from his bedroll, he raised to his knees to look for the Indians.

He heard a low whinny from his horse. He was surprised, as a ranger's horse was trained to be quiet in dangerous country. With the next flash, he made out a shape near his horse, but it was too indistinct to risk a shot. The muzzle blast of his rifle would disclose his position, and he was unwilling to do that while unsure of his target.

Motes kept his eyes fixed in the direction of the shape, his rifle ready. With the next lightning flash, he heard a bow string twang and an arrow thud into his saddle. Before the light was gone, he heard another twang from the direction of the shape, followed by the death scream of an Indian back by the tree where he had been sleeping.

Motes wondered why one Indian had shot another, but it was dark again before he could shoot. Again he heard the gentle whinny of his horse, but this time it was followed by a low whistle. Only Indian Jim, the rangers' faithful scout whistled like that!

Motes crawled through the darkness toward the shape he had been ready to shoot at. It was Indian Jim. They stayed in hiding all night, afraid other Indians might be near. Indian Jim whispered to Motes that he had stopped to camp, not knowing that the ranger was already there. It was seeing Indian Jim that made Motes' horse whinny so unexpectedly.

When daylight came they found a big Comanche with Indian Jim's arrow sticking all the way through his chest. The Comanche's arrow was embedded deep into Motes' saddle — a shot that would have killed Motes but for the death bird's warning.

The Comanche had hooted first, hoping some of his band were near. But the answering hoot had come from Indian Jim.

Suggested reading: Isaac Motes, "The Cry of the Death Bird," in *Frontier Times* (Bandera, Texas, October, 1923).

PLOW PUSHER

Pete Kitchen, the Daniel Boone of Arizona, came to the territory in 1854 when he was thirty-five. The Kentucky native had been a teamster in the War against Mexico and with the Mounted Rifles in their landmark journey from Fort Leavenworth to Fort Vancouver. He settled on the Santa Cruz River, south of Tucson.

The Santa Cruz Valley, running south sixty miles from Tucson to the Mexican border, was the most violent in Arizona. Hostile Apaches and settlers, both Mexican and American, waged constant war with each other. Every ranch nailed Apache ears to its gateposts, posting results of its battles.

The Indians burned Kitchen out in 1861, but he returned in a few years, settling midway between Calabasas and Nogales, six miles from the border. He had dreams of producing food on western land. He planted a thousand acres of fruit trees, vines, vegetables and grain. He ditched in irrigation water. He built up a large herd of cattle, and his three thousand hogs were the best bred swine west of St. Louis. It would take hard work to make barren land produce more than prickly pear, but Pete Kitchen could work.

He could also fight to defend his property. While Indians ridiculed him as a plow pusher, Kitchen built a fortified ranch house on a hill above El Potrero Creek. Armed sentries patrolled a walkway above the house, and a loaded rifle leaned against the wall at each porthole.

The Indians continued their attacks, and other settlers moved away until Kitchen was the only one within a hundred miles. His ranch became a haven in the ravaged valley. As soldiers and traders used the road that was once used by Father Kino and De Anza, they began calling it Pete Kitchen's road. His house, a citadel on a hill, became known for its open kitchen for friends and its open graveyard for Indians.

Kitchen's wife, Doña Rosa, set the finest table in Arizona. When General Crook brought the cavalry to Arizona, his officers and men were frequent guests. Besides food, they got good tips on fighting Apaches.

In 1870 Kitchen began hauling barley, potatoes and hogs to Tucson merchants. No longer would Tucson menus list only chili and venison for breakfast, chili and tamales for dinner, and plain chili for supper.

Kitchen took care to never follow the same route in

hauling his produce. Others were careless. Once he came upon the bodies of over twenty slaughtered Mexicans. He buried them on the spot. Sometimes the Indians, mad that they could not drive off Kitchen's hogs, filled them with so many arrows they looked like desert porcupines.

As Pete buried more Indians in his private cemetery, Doña Rosa would light candles at their graves and pray with her rosary. Athough she worried about burials with no ceremonial words, she was not afraid to add more graves in defense of home. When Indians attacked, she wrapped shirts around her legs to look like a man and took her place with rifle and a keen eye.

Some said Kitchen was a rough, charcoal sketch of a civilized man. Once he chased horse thieves into Mexico, killing one, and capturing another. He trussed the captive, threw him across the thief's own horse, and headed for home. That night Pete stopped for his first sleep in four nights on the trail. Before turning in, he sat the captive, hands and feet still tied, upright on the horse. Then he tied a rope to an overhead branch, dropping a noose over the captive's neck. Pete always enjoyed telling how surprised he was the next morning that "the damned hoss just wandered away to graze and left the feller a hangin' there."

In 1871 Pete's twelve-year-old adopted son, Crandall, was asleep on a haystack when Indians attacked. The boy knelt in prayer as bullets and arrows riddled him.

Pete carried his son's scalped body home and vowed to never retreat from his fight with Apache legions. He stayed, and the next year he marketed fourteen thousand pounds of bacon, five thousand pounds of lard, and wagon loads of fruit and vegetables. He had become the first big-scale farmer in the old West.

But when the railroad came through in 1882, bringing small farmers in its wake, Pete could no longer maintain his private army of friendly Opata Indians and his fortified citadel. He sold out, moved to Tucson, and died there in 1895, a legend of the old West at age seventy-three.

Suggested reading: Harold Preece, "Saga of the Amazing Pete Kitchen" in *Real West*, Vol. 6, no. 29 (May, 1963).

A BRAVE YOUNG MAN IN GRAND ISLAND

"I don't recollect his name," Mont Hawthorne said to his niece, "but he was the bravest man dying I ever did see. He was about twenty and I was barely twelve. I'd got back to Grand Island from helping Pa freight supplies into the Black Hills. Mama and my sisters had moved there from our homestead, while Pa and I was freighting. She was running the cattle corral to get a house to live in, and doing her nursing, too."

"Was that still in 1877?"

"Barely. Right on to Christmas and durned cold, too. Anyways, when this thing happened it took the Christmas spirit out of all of us. Right after the eastbound train pulled out that morning, a man came running to Mama, said there'd been a bad accident, and to bring her little brown bag.

"Fellow had ridden the brake rods all the way in from Sidney. He was 'most froze to death. When the train stopped, he crawled out to see if he could warm up and get something to eat. He was at the back of the Railroad House asking for leftovers when the train pulled out. He made a run for it, but he was still too froze to get his legs up out of the way. The wheels run over both of 'em, right up clost to his body."

"How awful!"

"A man who seen it ran right off for Doctor Gaines. He knowed Mama done nursing, so he got her, too. We got there first. They carried him into a carpenter shop for the doctor to look him over. The switchman had already tore off his own shirt, ripped it into rag strips and tied them around the thighs. But it didn't near stop the bleeding. The man didn't even whimper when they lifted him on to a plank and carried him into the shop and put him up on a workbench.

"The doctor couldn't do nothing for him. Him and Mama got fresh bandages on to keep him from bleeding too fast. The rest of us gathered up a bunch of fresh shavings and piled them around his hips and legs to soak up the blood and make it as soft as we could for him. There was no way on earth to save him and he knowed it as well as us."

"Did you know where he was going?"

"Iowa. The telegraph operator got his name and sent a message to his folks. He didn't want to worry them, but the operator sent it anyways. Then an answer come back. They said they would like to help, but they didn't have no money.

"The doctor had to go on and take care of other sick folks. He told Mama he was glad she was there. She promised to stay with him until the end.

"I'll never forget his eyes. They was big and a deep blue-black. He told Mama all about his whole life. He was the oldest of a big family. His folks was poor, so he got out soon's he could. He'd been clean to California, but times was tough all over then. He said thirty thousand men was out of work in Frisco alone. He couldn't get no work in Colorado, so he tried mining up in the Black Hills. He was coming back home, broke, when he got on the brake rods in Sidney.

"Just before the doctor left, the man asked if he could be set up and have a pine block to whittle on, as long as he was dying anyway. From the time the carpenter put that chunk of soft pine and a sharp jackknife into his hands, he never seemed to see nothing or nobody except that block he was whittling into shreds. The only times he would take his eyes off was to look at Mama, who was holding a cold cloth agin his head. Then he'd stop and rest a minute and take her hands and hold on tight and smile a little. He never whined or complained once. The reason I got to stay there was Mama needed me to bring cold water and run errands for her."

"How long did he last?"

"It was a long afternoon, I'll tell you. He never said nothin' to make anybody feel worse than they did already. Once he looked up at the carpenter and says, 'Am I keeping you from getting your work done?'

"He never made a face. He never let out a sound of pain. By late afternoon, them shavings was a mass of blood, and his hands was pure white. He was getting pretty weak, but he kept right on whittling as best he could.

"After he was too weak, Mama and the carpenter eased him back against some pillows she had me bring from our place. He held on to her hands and asked her to write his mother and tell her he'd done his best to get work so he could send money home. But ever place he'd been, they was too many ahead of him.

"He was talking too soft for anybody to hear him but mama. But she told me later what he said.

"After he was gone, Mama closed his eyes, laid him out straight, and wrapped her shawl around him. The carpenter made a coffin and they put the whittled piece of pine inside, right by him. Mama was glad she could write to his folks about having a nice coffin and a funeral and all.

"He sure was a brave young man."

Suggested reading: Martha F. McKeown, *Them Was The Days* (Lincoln: University of Nebraska Press, 1961).

COLORADO CANNIBAL

After his discharge from the Union Army in 1862, twenty-year-old Alferd Packer, a shoemaker, headed west to prospect. Eleven years later he was traveling from Utah to Colorado when his 21-man party became snowbound on the west slope of the San Juan Mountains. Chief Ouray of the Utes had warned the party about trying to cross the San Juans at that time of year. Nevertheless Packer and five others, Israel Swan, an Englishman named Bell, and three others, Humphreys, Miller and Moon, forged on ahead.

By the time they reached a plateau near present Lake City, Colorado, their food was gone, game was scarce, and the snow was deep. No one knows exactly what happened, but in April Packer showed up at Los Pinos Indian Agency on the Cochetopa River, almost dead from hunger and exposure.

When friends and relatives of the missing men got suspicious, the marshal at Saguache questioned Packer.

"What happened to the other five men?"

"Four of 'em headed south and Moon, he died in a blizzard."

"Where'd you get the money you been spending in the saloons?"

"Been working."

The marshal told Packer to guide a posse to the campsite. At first Packer led them astray. After threats by the marshal, Packer took them to the campsite where Powderhorn Creek meandered through a small plateau. The posse dug up what was left of five bodies. They had all been butchered.

Packer, his voice calm, said he'd been out hunting game. When he returned he found Bell alone and cooking some kind of meat.

"Where'd you get that?" I asked. "He looked like a crazy man. He grabbed his hatchet and charged right at me. I knew it was him or me, so I shot him. Then I looked around and saw all the others dead. They'd been killed by Bell with his hatchet. He'd cut some meat off Moon and that's what he was cooking."

He looked around at the posse. "Well what was I to do, starving and all? They was already dead. It wasn't so bad if you didn't think about what you was eating." He looked at them again as they shook their heads. "Well, what was I to do, being so hungry and the smell of the meat cooking?"

"Sure I took their money," he added. "You think I'd just let it lay there?"

Packer was arrested and taken to Lake City for trial. He escaped and wasn't found for nine years. He'd been living under a new name near Fort Fetterman in Wyoming.

In April, 1883, a Lake City jury found him guilty; he was sentenced to death. By then an important bit of evidence had been found. When the large party had become snowbound, Packer made several inquiries about how much money the five men were carrying. When he learned that Israel Swan had a lot of money, he tried to persuade Swan to go alone with him to look for help.

A common story claims that the trial judge said, "Packer, they was only six Democrats in Hinsdale County, and you done et five of 'em." Actually it was a saloon joke started by an observer at the trial.

Packer was taken to the Gunnison County jail to protect him from lynching and held there three years while he appealed his conviction. The Colorado Supreme Court reversed the conviction, probably because the circumstantial evidence was insufficient to prove malice as required for murder.

Packer got a change of venue for his new trial to Gunnison County. Again, he was again found guilty, this time on five counts of manslaughter. The judge sentenced him to forty years. At his age this was virtually a life sentence.

Harry Tammen and Fred Bonfils, publishers of the *Denver Post*, started a newspaper campaign to free Packer. He was released in 1901.

When it was learned that the publishers had planned to exhibit Packer in a circus, a lawyer, William "Plug Hat" Anderson, shot and wounded both men. Anderson was tried three times before he won his acquittal. At one of the trials the judge said, "Plug Hat, your motive was admirable, but your marksmanship abominable."

Packer died five years after his release, five years of drifting around the country, shunned by all.

If you climb toward Slumgullian Pass near Lake City you will reach a small plateau, where Powderhorn Creek flows quietly through. It is marked on many maps, "Cannibal Plateau."

Suggested reading: E. Ward McCray, "Man-Eater of Powderhorn Creek," in *Old West, v. 1, no. 2* (Winter, 1964).

TALL LADDER

Will Rogers and Willard Ripley, finding no riches in the Black Hills of South Dakota, moved west to Wyoming to homestead. Rogers filed a claim about five miles north of Devils Tower and Ripley settled just to his east.

Money was hard to come by. The settlers looked up at the 865-foot, fluted rock shaft, resembling a tall tree stump, and wondered.

"Nobody's ever climbed it," Rogers said.

"Mebbe we could make money outa being first."

"How'd we ever get up?"

"How about drivin' wooden poles into one of them narrow cracks. See where they run all the way up?"

"You mean, make a ladder?"

"Why not?"

"The damn thing's near nine hundred feet high."

"I figure it can't be more'n about three fifty in the straight up and down part. Besides, we only gotta make one step at a time."

"Hell, let's give it a try."

It was spring 1893 before their plans were complete. By June they had cut hundreds of three-foot long stakes, mostly from ash, willow, and oak timber in the hills. They hauled them as close to the base of the tower as they could with a team and wagon. They had to carry them by hand for the last quarter-mile over loose rock and small cliffs.

Each stake had to be driven into the crack with a heavy hammer. Balancing on the top driven stake while holding the next stake with one hand and swinging the hammer with the other was precarious. Neither man had any experience mountaineering, but being broke is a great motivation.

Their progress was slow. Each night they returned to their claims to do chores. They had more confidence in their new venture than in raising crops in the thin Wyoming soil.

After a section of four or five steps had been driven in, they sawed the ends off flush and nailed a two by four to them. This served as the handrail for their shaky ladder. As they worked higher and higher the narrow crack began to curve. Now construction became much more difficult. Each step was offset from the one below, and the handrail no longer ran straight up and down. But Ripley was left-handed and the way the crack curved gave him an advantage. So he worked at the top and Rogers brought up the new stakes.

They had chosen the southwest side of the tower. Some days the temperature went over a hundred. Hanging on to a stake with one sweaty hand and swinging the hammer with another presented new challenges.

Shortly after starting construction, Rogers wrote to newspapers in the Black Hills, saying they would have a Fourth of July celebration. They planned a demonstration ascent with refreshments and entertainment at the bottom. Both men hoped they'd be ready and that people would come.

The experience of building the giant ladder along the sheer part of the tower made the climb on to the top seem like child's play.

Rogers is usually given credit for being the first to reach the top. But Ripley's backers point out that the left-handed man would have been logically the first one to go on up.

The nearest towns were Rapid City and Deadwood, over 125 miles away. A crowd estimated from 1000 to 3000 made the ten-day round trip. Most arrived on July 3 and camped out, as there were no overnight accommodations.

Stands for viewers were built. Rogers and Ripley planned to make their money on entertainment and refreshments. The climb was a free attraction. The entertainment started with a dance on July 3.

To keep the spirit of the holiday they decided to carry an American flag to the top. They couldn't find one large enough, so they got a local artist to paint stars and stripes on a large sheet of cloth.

A light rain fell on the third, and people worried. But the Fourth dawned bright and clear. Rogers carried the flag to the top and set it up. A wind came up in the afternoon and blew it over. It floated down, dropping among the celebrants below. Rogers and Ripley, recognizing their opportunity, cut up the flag. They sold the stars at fifty cents each and small pieces of the stripes went for twenty-five.

Devils Tower has been scaled many times by mountaineers using traditional rock climbing methods. But those ascents lacked the flair and the profitability of the first spectacular climb.

Suggested reading: Raymond McIntyre, The First White Men on Devils Tower, in *Frontier Times, v. 42, no. 5,* (September, 1968).

60

THE KILLING OF THE APACHE KID

An Apache the whites called The Apache Kid terrorized the New Mexico frontier during the last of the territorial days. The most wanted outlaw in the territory, he made his last raid on September 20, 1907, when he stole horses and destroyed property on the James Brothers ranch forty-five miles from Hot Springs. A posse from the ranch chased him, got close enough for the Kid to shoot at them, and then gave up. They returned to Fairview to report what had happened.

Burt Slinkard, who had a saloon in Fairview, was in the new posse that went after the Kid. The others were Bill Keene, Sebe Sorrells, Mike Sullivan, and Walter Hern. None of them ever said much about how they caught and killed the Kid.

Slinkard married the mother of Susan Lee in 1913. Seven years later Susan asked him who killed the Kid. She had heard many versions, most of them different. Burt had never talked about it.

"I don't know and neither does anyone else," Burt replied.

"Well you were there, so why don't you know?"

Then Burt told the story.

They had trailed the Kid into the San Mateo Mountains. They saw his campfire as it grew dark. Bill Keene, an older man, was selected as the leader. He set out these rules:

There was to be no harm to any women or children in the Kid's camp. They should watch carefully to avoid ambush. Walter Hern would stay with the horses. The other three would stay in sight of each other as they slipped up on the camp, so that when Bill gave the signal to shoot, all could shoot together.

When the men crawled up within range, they saw a cooking pot on the fire. The Kid came out of his shelter from time to time to tend his fire, but his oldest son was with him each time, and Bill did not signal to shoot. They never had a clear shot at the Kid when his son was not also close by, so the posse watched all night and never fired a shot.

At daybreak the Kid and the boy came out again, but this time the Kid sent the boy after their horses. Then he turned and walked to the campfire alone. Keene gave the signal, four shots rang out, and the Kid fell. The Kid's woman and other children ran from the shelter and escaped.

Then the posse went down to the shelter and saw that

the Kid had been hit twice.

"That's why I don't know who killed him," Burt told Susan. "Four of us shot and two missed. I only hope it wasn't me hit him. If I did, it was an accident, because I was scared and not too good a shot. I was pretty young and had no experience with Indians. Common sense would say it was Bill Keene and Sebe Sorrels. They were both level headed and fine shots. All I hope is it wasn't me."

"Why did you feel that way?" Susan asked. "He was a menace to every family in the territory. He killed everybody he could. You were protecting women and children left alone on ranches."

"We thought we were trailing a well-armed renegade. You know, risking our lives. The other posse said he'd shot at them. But he didn't have a decent cartridge in his camp. He did have some powder and casings where he had poured powder in and shoved a bullet down. We found his old gun and fired one of the homemade cartridges. It made a good noise, but the bullet barely got out of the barrel before it dropped to the ground. If he'd had decent ammunition he would have ambushed that whole first posse.

"I don't like the idea of ambushing an unarmed man, and that's what we did. I didn't feel proud about it, and I don't like to talk about it."

"You brought Mom the ring and bracelet and arrows from his camp."

"Yeah, I did that. His woman and kids had scattered into the brush. I guess that was stealing, but I didn't think too much about it, compared with shooting an unarmed man from ambush." He paused. "In fact I was going to bring back the cooking pot, too, but it was so heavy. I put it down and planned to go back for it, but I never did."

"But everyone in the territory was mighty thankful that your posse got rid of the worst bandit in the country."

"Any ten-year-old kid with a decent gun could have done what we did — ambushing an unarmed man. I don't want to talk about it any more."

Suggested reading: Susan E. Lee, *These Also Served* (Los Lunas, New Mexico: Priv. Publ., 1960).

ORDERING INFORMATION

True Tales of the Old West is projected for 36 volumes.

Proposed titles include:

Warriors and Chiefs	In print
Soldiers	In print
Native Women	In print
Mountain Men	In print
Pioneer Women	In print
Ranchers and Cowboys	In print
Horses and Riders	In print
Miners	In print
Entertainers	In print
Dogs and Masters	In print
Outlaws	In print
Frontiersmen	In print
Lawmen	Soon to appear
Gamblers	Soon to appear
Homesteaders	Soon to appear
Explorers	Under way
Lawyers & Judges	Under way
Scouts	Under way
Writers	Under way
Railroaders	Started
Merchants	Started
Army Women	Started
Vigilantes	Started

Ask at your bookstore or write:

PIONEER PRESS
Box 216
Carson City, NV 89702-0216